Life in Miniatures

a view from the piano bench

Life in Miniatures

a view from the piano bench

Carol Rich

ISBN: 9798700730488
Edited by Franny French
Cover design by Anita Jones of Another Jones Graphics

For my father

If I had influence with the good fairy,
I would ask that her gift to each child be
a sense of wonder so indestructible
that it would last throughout life.

Rachel Carson

Acknowledgments

My deepest gratitude to Franny French, editor and friend, whose commitment and insight never waver.

Special thanks to Anita Jones of Another Jones Graphics for creating a cover design she seemingly drew out from the depths of my mind.

My heartfelt thanks goes out to my teachers, whose words of wisdom continue to profoundly influence every aspect of my life. I've tried to be as kind and generous with my students as you were with me.

To my readers Michael Carroll and Marijo C. Brantner, thank you for your candor, expertise, and friendship. Patricia Hauschildt, your input in the final stages of the manuscript was invaluable. Your writer's eye for detail is matched by your musician's ear for phrasing.

Thanks also to Lisa C. Knisely for her advice and encouragement in the early stages of *Life in Miniatures: a view from the piano bench.*

To David Biespiel, who I "met" only one time on a ten-minute phone call, thank you for sharing your enthusiasm and wisdom with me, a total stranger. It made all the difference.

As always, my deepest love and gratitude to the love of my life, my wife, Georgia Arrow.

Table of Contents

Life in Miniatures

a view from the piano bench

Part One

Carol Rich

On Being a Pianist

There's a photo of me playing piano when I was three years old. It's a black and white, but I have a clear memory of the ruffled pink dress I was wearing. The shoes were Buster Browns with straps across the top that closed with a loop and button. I didn't know exactly how it worked—I was only three—but I do remember holding the silver hooking device in my clenched fist.

In the photo, my legs dangle from the bench and cross nonchalantly at the ankle. My fingers splay over the keys like the ungainly legs of a baby giraffe. My face frowns in concentration as I glare at my father, the photographer. My expression says, "Don't bother me, Dad. I'm practicing." My fingers say, "We've no idea what we're doing, but we want to do this forever."

The Steinway in the photo, my lifelong companion, was built in Hamburg in 1913 and purchased at the New York factory by Birdie, my father's mother. In 1958, when I first lifted my hands to the keys, it became mine.

Shanta 66

My presents under the tree could wait. First, I had to find the unwrapped, unlabeled gift that was hiding somewhere among the Ukrainian ornaments, porcelain bells, and strings of beaded cranberries. It would masquerade as an animal ornament, and it would be new. It would be for me. The tinsel my brother Bob had placed on the branches one strand at a time made my search challenging, but eventually, I spotted a small, curved, gray trunk poking out from behind a bell. The elephant's back was draped in a red blanket with the name Shanta embroidered on it in gold thread. I loved the way its trunk curled under my thumb when I cupped it in my hands. Shanta 66 was the last in a long line of miniature stuffed animals Bob would hang on the Christmas tree for me. I was eleven. He was thirteen.

In previous years, I'd gotten a ladybug, tiger, dog, and furry spider. One year, I got an actual stuffed duckling, not fake. Our fox terrier, Scrappy, turned it into a small carpet of yellow feathers encrusted with hardened beak, leg, and toe bits. Tim, my Teddy bear from Grandma, held my hand while the duckling got vacuumed up.

Bob had spoken about his secret gifts only once when I found a four-inch tall, tinsel-haired giraffe balanced on a string of blue beads. When I reached up to take it, Bob cupped his hand to my ear and whispered, "Merry Christmas, sis."

Finding North

Dad opened the front door to a wall of packed snow topped with six inches of neon blue sky. Squinting into the glare, I shifted in my snow boots and zipped my snowsuit. Our best escape would be through the garage door that sat at the bottom of an incline. The snow there would be more like a hillside than a mountainside; it'd be slippery, but we'd be able to clamber out. Dad led the way, followed by my brothers Ken and Bob, and finally me. After we were out, but before we were allowed to play, Dad and the boys shoveled a tunnel-path all the way from the front door to the street. I was happy to follow from behind, and used my kid-size shovel to remove snow clumps that tumbled like miniature landslides off the tunnel walls.

Afterwards, while my brothers pummeled one another with snowballs in the backyard, I looked for shapes in snowdrifts in the front that could be made into something interesting like a ship or a fort. I'd want a place to hide when my brothers tired of each other and decided they needed a sister-target. It was sure to happen when I least expected it—hard-packed snow missiles would zero in on me from two directions at once, making it impossible to avoid being hit. They called it "crossfire."

For a while at least, I was alone with the virgin snow. I climbed a tall, white mound, plopped down on my butt, and held my breath as I listened to the muted acoustics of my refuge.

Handholds

I was in fifth grade. Admittedly, many of my childhood memories are shrouded in uncertainty or have been buried under layers of emotional dust, but I remember that year specifically because the middle school was under construction and our classes were held in the Methodist church across the street.

The sky had been spitting snowflakes all morning, but not enough to get excited about. I cleared my fogged-up glasses, tightened the rubber bands on my pigtails, and copied equations off the board.

Suddenly, the daylight was sucked out of the room. I wondered if there was a power outage, but the teacher grinned, flipped on the overhead lights, and motioned for us to continue working. I wriggled in my seat and scribbled down the homework due on Monday. Math was my favorite subject and Mr. Tina was my favorite teacher. Math was the first thing I did when I got home from school; it came before having a snack, playing outside, and even practicing piano.

All of a sudden, huge snowflakes were plummeting past the windows. A student runner came in with a note for Mr. Tina. Several kids reached for their backpacks, but he held up his hand and fake-glared. "Wait . . ." he said. He sat at his desk and slowly opened a book. "Just kidding! Now you may leave." He slammed the book shut, and the classroom erupted with sounds of chairs scraping across the floor and kids scrambling for the exit. Everyone dispersed into the thickening whiteness, and before I had time to pull on my coat, I was alone.

Early release meant no school bus, and Mom would never venture out into the weather to pick me up. There'd be homemade cookies and hot chocolate when I got home, but the slightest film of white on the road and she'd be housebound. The only time I ever saw her choose to go out into the snow was the day she bolted from the kitchen and ran, wide-eyed and red-faced, out the front door. No hat, no coat, no scarf—just a Mom-on-fire running like a disoriented rabbit into a howling snowstorm. Hours later, she returned shivering and wet. "Hot flashes," Dad mumbled.

As I pieced together a plan to get home, I wondered if my teary-eyed Mom was peering through the picture window in hopes of seeing me bounding up the front path. Bob wasn't anywhere around, and Ken was in high school, miles away; he wouldn't have looked for me anyway. There was no plan for this. It was only a couple of miles to get home. I'd have to hoof it.

I had a terrific winter hat collection, and I felt lucky that my hat of the day was the purple and white striped one. I pulled it down low over my eyebrows, threw my schoolbag over my shoulder, and began the trek home.

Stepping outside, I was startled by the absolute silence that engulfed me. Snow plummeted toward the earth with such urgency—it was incomprehensible that there was no resulting sound. The giant flakes fell so close together and landed so contentedly, they created the sort of purposeful quiet that eased into my bones, especially if I closed my eyes to listen. It was like that moment right before lifting my hands to play Chopin.

Flakes landed on my eyelashes, and when I lifted my foggy glasses with the thumb of my mitten, tiny bits of ice hit my eyelids. I had to get moving. I wondered why I hadn't put on my snow boots that morning. Rain boots had no traction whatsoever and made every step on the upward-slanting hill tricky. The biggest challenge would be Western Drive, the street where I lived. It was a *real* hill, known as the best sledding spot in town. It was also a dead end, notorious for not being plowed.

The first few blocks were manageable, and my mood lifted. I kept to where the grass grew and used the occasional branch and street sign as handholds. But the snow was accumulating fast, and my toes were already cold.

I listened; I ignored my toes; I found my rhythm.

While I was maneuvering across a slippery side street, something streaked in front of me and disappeared into a bush. There was another one—*zing*—and another. Snowballs. A group of boys was scrambling up the hill behind me, like a pack of blood-thirsty wolves zeroing in on their prey.

Then I got hit hard. My cheek stung and snow clumped under my collar before sliding inside my shirt and down my back. Every inch of my body was wet with sweat. I got hit again, this time on the arm. Two more rockets flew past and then one hit squarely on my bag, knocking it to the ground. The guys had pretty bad aim, considering how many snowballs they hefted at me. Still, icy drops of wetness gathered at my chin. They itched and stung like tiny needles.

"Hey! Leave her alone!"

It was Bob. He was alone—one boy against three or four. Snowballs were cradled in the crook of his arm. One was raised over his head, ready to launch.

"I mean it, get out of here!"

One more snowball flew past, but that was it. My chest heaved as it took in lungfuls of frigid air. I brushed off my pants and coat, and then Bob fished my schoolbag out of the snow and threw it over my shoulder. He gently ran his finger across the sore spot on my cheek and straightened my purple and white striped hat. He flicked the big white pompom on top and smiled.

Then he took my hand.

Carol Rich

Banned From Heaven

My childhood friend Pam and her four older sisters were inside hanging the pasta that their mom, Flora, had made from scratch. Ribbons of dough were draped from special wooden drying racks as well as from every available rod, handle, and chair back. The first time I'd seen it, I thought that the uncooked pasta looked like flat filaments of pasty, flabby, raw chicken. Flour was strewn about the floor, counters, and atop Flora's sloppily bunned hair.

Pam and I escaped the flour-explosion zone by taking our lemonades outside to play Seven-Up against the heavily textured stucco wall on the side of the house. Bounce against the wall six times and catch; bounce against the wall and then the pavement and catch; bounce, clap and catch; bounce, clap five times, and catch. The progressively challenging tasks elicited more intense laughter the harder they got, especially when a deep groove in the stucco caught the blue rubber ball and ripped it to the side or straight at our faces.

We rode bikes for the rest of the afternoon, zipping down the street, up onto sloped driveways, onto sidewalks, and all over again. Hers was a too-tall red bike; mine, a metallic blue one that rattled loudly from the slightest crack or rise in the pavement. Ours was a friendship of laughter and unexpected turns.

One day, Mom took me aside and told me I couldn't be friends with Pam anymore, that her family was no longer Italian Catholic. They'd converted to being Jehovah's Witnesses. "What? They're not

Italian anymore?" I asked. Mom averted her eyes when she told me Flora thought I was a bad influence on Pam—that I'd drag her down to hell with me.

After that, I met with Pam and a woman named Louisa, who, even though they knew I was there covertly, included me in their weekly study group. I tried not to imagine how red Mom's face would get and how thin and tight her lips would become if she ever found out I was going behind her back. It was clear to me that seeing Pam after being told not to was an act of premeditated deception. My lie felt black, but also intriguing and liberating.

I continued to feign interest in Pam's and Louisa's desire to save my soul. In reality, I went to be near my best friend. Plus, my pulse raced and my face got hot whenever Louisa leaned over me to point out a passage in the white, zip-up, red-letter Bible Mom and Dad had given me when I was little.

One day, Louisa stopped me at the threshold of Pam's house. I'd been banned. Finding myself standing alone on the front stoop, I stared at the brass lion door knocker. Every fiber in my being knew that Mom, not Flora, was behind my banishment.

I hopped on my bike and raced straight home, ignoring the sizzling anger in my gut.

Carol Rich

Mountain Ranges

My father's hands hover over the keyboard next to mine. We're playing four-hand music.

His were perfectly sculpted pianist's hands, shaped for agility and coverage. They were also "soft hands," a term pianists use to mean having sensitivity to nuance, color, and tone. From my vantage point, the landscape of his hands—the knuckles, joints, and veins—resembled mountain ranges. The memory is a snapshot, a still life depicting twelve years of making music together.

Because I started playing when I was only three, sight-reading was instinctive—like breathing. Music was my native language. English ranked second, something in need of constant vigilance and correction. Music is direct.

I learned the entire symphonic repertoire while sitting on the piano bench beside my father. While we progressed through the works of Haydn, Mozart, Beethoven, Schubert, Schumann, Brahms, and Tchaikovsky, I learned how to truly listen, how to bend to harmonic need, how to voice and balance, how to make my part sound like soaring violins or a choir of trombones, and how to give character to the notes on the page—all on the first read-through. I discovered a river of music flowing through me, like joy in my veins.

Bertha Mandelbaum

Bertha Mandelbaum Rich, Birdie to us kids, was a petite woman. Everything she wore was neatly pressed and perfectly fitted. She had pearls for every outfit. Her eyes smiled when she talked, and her half-glasses dangled from her hand as if to substantiate her point of view. She studied at Juilliard before it was Juilliard, when it was called the Institute of Musical Art. She represented my musical heritage, but aside from showing a vague interest in my piano lessons, she kept me at a chilly distance. I don't remember ever having been hugged by her. My heart was constantly sore from wanting more.

Milton Rich, or Bumpah, as we knew him, was a Mason, so we were always eyeballing the mysterious symbols imprinted on the oddly shaped items in the apartment. I particularly liked a tiny gold trowel with an engraving of an eye positioned in the middle of a triangle. All I remember of Bumpah was his hefty size, his wide smile, his business suits that had a gold chain hanging from an inside pocket, and sitting quietly on his knee while the adults talked.

Their Upper East Side apartment was tastefully furnished with things you couldn't touch, sit on, or play with. However, there was a tall, glass and gold curio cabinet filled with shiny, bejeweled trinkets we kids *could* play with, if we asked politely. Bob and I favored a fish that flexed at several joints, which, when they moved, gave it a sparkly, slithery look. A tiny clasp opened its stomach, but nothing was ever inside.

ꕥ

Most pianists I've known have had a turning-point piece of music that ignites an inextinguishable thirst to play. Mine was the G Minor Ballade by Chopin, which, in conjunction with Chopin's *Revolutionary* Etude, I learned during my sophomore year in high school. The advanced repertoire signaled that I'd entered the next echelon of being a serious musician.

One day it occurred to me, or more accurately, a subconscious bubble finally surfaced, that Birdie would have amazing stories to tell about her time at Juilliard. I sent her a letter asking about her musical background. It was quite brazen to ask for personal information from my grandmother, especially without approval from my parents. My reasoning was that if I could play difficult repertoire, I could write a personal letter to Birdie. I received a three-page, single-spaced letter typewritten on expensive-looking translucent paper that crinkled when I held it.

Darling, your card arrived yesterday and with it your dear letter from which I got a real thrill reading about your love of the Ballade in G minor, one of my very own favorites! . . . The Revolutionary Etude is a magnificent left hand study, but after you have worked with it a while why not put it away for a bit and instead take up the Prelude in E-flat by Rachmaninoff or Fairy Tale by Medtner, both of which are equally fine studies for the left hand.

I played for [Arthur Fiedler] and had dinner at their home in Boston years ago. He had a very beautiful wife and he was charming and very complimentary about my playing. I also met the great conductor Koussevitzky at that time and the Russian composer, Glazunov. . . . I also had some visits [lessons] with Prokofiev when he came to the U. S. He was a tall, blond Russian but spoke English quite well. . . . I knew Efrem Zimbalist. . . . His son is now a film producer I think.

Birdie knew the revered Bach specialist Rosalyn Tureck and harpsichordist Wanda Landowska. And in Birdie's own words, she also played for "Marian Anderson, the Negro contralto who preceded and followed us." She shared stories about playing the Grieg and Tchaikovsky piano concertos with the Chicago Symphony.

Well then I met my darling Milt and after two years we had to move to Minneapolis. I played chamber music with men from the Orchestra there and could have been soloist with the orchestra, but your Daddy was on the way and I stopped all music for a while. (What a blessing he has been to me and how fortunate I am to have such a fine son and natural born musician at that! I always wished I had his ability to play "by ear" as they call it.)

Birdie studied with Rafael Joseffy, the famous editor of Chopin manuscripts, and also with Van Cliburn's teacher, Rosina Lhévinne. Birdie's words about her inspired me for years.

I also had the joy of studying with Rosina Lhévinne, not at Juilliard but at her home and that was the best instruction I had ever received, the most natural hand positions, etc. I think she was the greater of the two. . . . (referring to Rosina's husband, the legendary Josef Lhévinne) . . . *but she said having one great performing artist in the family was sufficient, although they gave many two-piano recitals together. I liked him too but stood in awe of his prodigious technique. Meanwhile, all through the years I had made the great composers my bosom friends. . . .*

I was stunned by my grandmother's interaction with so many musical giants, and I was shocked—staggered—by how far she'd taken her solo career. I was also infuriated. She'd kept this rich heritage from me. I'd never have known about it if I hadn't asked. She seemed to relish sharing her stories with me. Where was this woman while I was growing up? What or who had gotten in our way?

❧

I waited a premeditated six years to send a letter to Rosina Lhévinne. But in the meantime, I graduated from high school and completed my Bachelor of Music degree from the Hartt School of Music. It wasn't until then that, with my teacher's encouragement, I asked for a private audition with Mme. Lhévinne, three months ahead of my Juilliard Masters audition. In my letter, I mentioned that my grandmother had studied with her, and that my father had studied organ at Juilliard. I revealed my admiration of her legendary teaching style and how honored I'd be to play for her. Contacting Mme. Lhévinne occurred at a critical juncture in my life, and my future hinged on her response. The envelope was returned to me unopened. **Deceased** was written across the front in thick black ink.

ঌ

The last paragraph of Birdie's letter read,

No doubt your mother and dad will think I have gone out of my mind to write you all this, but it is the answer to your question. Please write soon again and forgive me if I have tired you. I promise this is the first and last time. All my dearest love to you.

She hand signed it, "Birdie," with two happy eighth notes embellishing the "e."

She died of breast cancer the following year.

Curtain's Up!

Most Saturdays, Dad took me to the New York Public Library. While he loaded up on reading material, I rummaged through the stacks of LPs. The first rule of the game was that I was allowed to take home as many records as my arms could carry. The second was that I had to select an eclectic mix of music. Lastly, I had to listen to everything I'd chosen. The game familiarized me with all genres of classical music including opera, choral, solo instrumental, vocal *lied,* symphonic, chamber music, and of course, keyboard repertoire, which included recordings of Rosalyn Tureck and Wanda Landowska. Dad gave his silent blessing to the occasional jazz record that made it into my pile. I loved it all.

When I turned twelve, Dad deemed that I could attend my first opera. I'd seen the New York Philharmonic at Philharmonic Hall and ballets at the New York State Theater. But all I knew of the Metropolitan Opera House were two colorful thirty-foot by thirty-six-foot murals by Marc Chagall visible from the outside, through the building's gargantuan glass walls.

I'd been to Lincoln Center only in daylight, and when Dad led me through the throngs of perfumed, bejeweled, nighttime concert-goers, I felt like I'd entered a forbidden, enchanted world. The sprawling plaza and its landmark fountain glowed with golden light. The very walls of the performance venues seemed to swell with energy.

Inside the Met, luxuriousness oozed from the carpets, staircases, and ceilings. I counted three galaxy-like lobby chandeliers, and five balconies inside the hall. Our seats were in the second row, right behind the conductor. Although most halls left the first rows of patrons looking up the noses and skirts of the performers, the Met was so vast, we could see everything on stage, right down to the buckles on the singers' shoes.

When the lights dimmed, everyone around us turned to watch the hall's massive Sputnik-like chandelier rise up into the ceiling. During the overture, I watched the weaving, bobbing heads of the musicians in the pit. (Little did I know at the time that I'd spend much of my musical life in Portland, Oregon, playing in the pit—albeit a cramped, stinky, stuffy one.) I swooned over the Metropolitan Opera Orchestra and its Brillo-haired conductor, James Levine. The soaring melodies were familiar to me. I'd been listening to them for a week. Yet, a recording couldn't prepare me for the lushness of sound, breadth of phrasing, and clarity of tone that came from that orchestra. I could hardly breathe. Then the curtain went up.

The opera was *Salome,* by Richard Strauss. Considering the dangerously seductive nature of the female lead, it's astonishing that Dad chose it as my first foray into opera. I cowered in my seat when John the Baptist's head was carried out on a silver platter and presented center stage—directly in front of me. It was grotesque and bloody, and extremely lifelike. I couldn't look away. It was so cool.

Then came The Dance of the Seven Veils. Who wouldn't love seven scantily dressed nymphs dancing seductively just for you?

That same season, Dad took me to *Der Rosenkavalier,* also by Strauss. When the curtain went up, it took me a minute to find the action on stage. But when I did, it was the most startling, most titillating moment of my life. Two women were making love in an oversized bed, right there in front of me *and* the stuffy Metropolitan Opera audience. One of the women, the earthy and alluring Christa Ludwig, sang the part of Octavian, a "pant" role, which revealed the unique richness and register of her alto voice. Ludwig's vocal timbre and physique sent multiple tremors through my body. I swooned. I sighed. I fell profoundly in love with Strauss.

Throughout the four-plus hours of the opera, I was spellbound, and relished every nuance of role play. The blending of Christa Ludwig's luscious golden tone with the ethereally silver soprano voice of Teresa Stich-Randall, who played Sofie, the object of Octavian's love, roused and satisfied musical desires I didn't know I had. I succumbed to the profound allure of first love. But at the time, my own youth prevented me from fully appreciating the stately, all-knowing Marschallin, who inhabited the body and voice of Elisabeth Schwarzkopf. The final trio and duet lifted my heart clear out of my chest. It was the night I lost my musical virginity.

Carol Rich

The Mirror

Particles rained like stardust onto my sleeping teenage body. The sensation was evocative, but the dream was interrupted by the odd sound of scraping, which was followed by something heavy rolling across the floor. The thing wobbled like a coin on a table; it quivered faster and faster until its edges closed in on a full stop by the head of my bed. Looking down, I saw my distorted expression gawking back at me from the wavy complexion of the glass in my gold-rimmed mirror. The wire at the back was still intact. I re-hung it on its nail and went back to sleep.

The same thing happened the next night: a pleasant sensation of ghostly stardust, a scraping and rolling noise, wobbling, and me looking down at myself in the mirror. The wire was still intact, but a piece of the two-inch wide, gold veneer on the rim was chipped.

The third time it happened, the sound of the rolling mirror was coupled with the evocative sensation. I reattached the mirror with a cup hook. If it happened again, I'd dub the mirror haunted and put it at the back of the closet.

A few nights later, I heard it slide down the wall, and I woke up a second sooner, in time to see it wobble to a stop next to my bed. Throwing off the covers, I ran to the wall. The cup hook faced downward. The wire on the back of the mirror was intact, and another piece of gold veneer was missing. I put the mirror in the closet and never had the floating-poltergeist-stardust dream again.

Betrayal

The ranch house in which I grew up had a huge multi-purpose basement. There was a workshop, laundry room, spare bedroom—which had Ken's dried booger collection spattered about on the wallpaper—and a storage area where Dad kept an elaborate train setup and a collection of paperback mysteries displayed in alphabetical order against the entire back wall. The main area of the basement was a playroom with a TV, a card table for jigsaw puzzles, a dartboard, a full-size chalkboard where I'd create color pictures of The Beatles while I watched them play on The Ed Sullivan Show, and my black and white rocking horse that was attached to a stand with long, stretched-out springs. When I was nine, I got a fully decked-out Annie Oakley outfit and rode that rocking horse for hours—but never after dark when an elongated face pattern in the paneling appeared directly behind me.

We also had a fold-up ping pong table. All of the Riches, except for Mom, were expert ping pong players. Dad had a fancy paddle from Japan that had smooth thick red rubber padding. Ping pong was one of the few activities I enjoyed playing with both of my brothers. Still, every now and then, just to keep me in my place, Ken liked to remind me that since I was the "special" one—the youngest, the only girl, the one Dad bonded with through music—I didn't deserve any other happiness. Ever.

One day, it was up to Ken and me to put the fold-up table away into the workshop. He was four years older than me, and I was still a little kid. But it wasn't hard to fold the table, and even though it towered over me, it was on wheels, so it was relatively easy to move. As usual, we pushed it into the workshop, but instead of nestling it against the back wall, my brother tipped the table toward me. It was off its wheels, and suddenly I was being crushed under its weight. There was no way I could get it upright by myself, and it took all my might just to keep it stationary. It shifted on the floor, but I knew if I let go, I'd be crushed. I cried out to my brother for help, but then the lights went out and the door slammed shut. I cried out again, louder this time. My arms shook. Tears and snot ran down my face and into my mouth. Images of workshop things, things my brother had kicked awake when he abandoned me there, loomed bigger in the dark: my father's power tools, boxes of electrical equipment, and things I couldn't identify even in the light—all kinds of dangerous contraptions—some that might morph into monsters eager to sink their teeth into me, grab at my feet, claw at my hair, and pin me to the floor with their knees sinking into my stomach.

A wave of nausea passed through me. I squeezed my eyes shut and tried to remember where things were, and for the first time in my life, I realized I had to save myself. It wasn't bravery. I had no choice. It took one exhausting, muscle-straining inch at a time, but I managed to slide out from beneath the table. When I finally pushed my puny body clear, the table crashed to the floor, where it knocked into something that rolled across the cement and landed with a *thud* against the wall. I didn't smell anything noxious, but I hoped whatever it was wouldn't ooze under my knees and hands.

I was freed, yet I had no sense of where the door was. And now, the ping pong table was lying flat on its side, possibly blocking the exit. It would make crawling out that much harder. The undersized toolkit Dad had given me was next to the fishing rods in the corner. I'd hate to knock those over. Bob's chemistry set was somewhere around too. I had to avoid the bottle of sulfur that made the basement stink whenever there was a botched experiment.

My foot was wedged against something solid. I felt it with my hand and I froze. It was the Box of the Dead—the one thing that was off-limits—and I was touching it in the dark. Quickly, I retracted my hand.

Once, my father showed us kids the contents of the heavy wooden box that was piled up with things he'd gathered in the war. His mouth tightened when he told us that he'd kept the stuff to honor dead German soldiers. I never learned whether he'd actually killed the soldiers he was honoring. My father was a musician and a pacifist. I didn't understand why he had German weapons, a Nazi patch, and other war "souvenirs."

I kept my foot against the box as a point of reference. If I could find another landmark, I could figure out where the door was. Inching my fingers along the rough cement floor, I tried to avoid running my hand into the sharp-edged metal legs of the table saw, or the shelves stacked with paint cans and power tools. I cried out again, but my voice was trapped inside the workshop with me.

Then I bumped into the ping pong table. I pivoted on my knees. I suspected the door was right in front of me. As I reached out, my fingers landed on something cold and hard. I jumped back and hit my head on the bottom of the table saw. Pain shot through my eye. In a flash, I knew what I'd touched: a German luger in the Box of the Dead. My throat constricted and I scooted away from the box as fast as I could. My shoulder hit the corner of the workbench. I was right by the door! Reaching up, I twisted the doorknob, and tumbled onto the floor in the playroom. The lights were off in there too, and the curtains were drawn.

As I sat on the linoleum tile floor at the foot of the stairs, my head reeled from a tornado-like rush of memories—freakish incidents which had occurred in that stairwell: our first dog, a Dalmatian named Trixie, slip-sliding down the stairs after my brothers had attached roller skates to her skinny paws; me, running down the stairs and getting my fingers caught in the wrought iron filigree of the railing; my tight-lipped father dragging Ken by the ear, kicking and screaming all the way up the stairs after he'd plugged up the shower drain with a facecloth to see how high the water would go; Scrappy moaning at the top of the stairs, her stomach visibly convulsing from having eaten two tubes of blue and green oil paint; my silver Slinky propelling itself—suicide-style—off the top step. In my mind, it was still tumbling and lurching like a clunky, doubly decapitated caterpillar, down to where I was resting.

When I scrambled up to the kitchen, my brother/monster was sitting at the table reading a book and eating a tuna sandwich.

Baby Great Horned Owl and the Murder of Crows

The din of crows was the first thing to greet me when I entered the woods. Gathering high up in the canopy, the *Corvids* were parenthetical—like clouds or distant traffic noise. I concentrated on the finer sounds and movements in the trees.

It was late March. Owl fledgling season. I knew that crystalizing the image of an owl in my mind's eye would increase my chances of seeing one. Stillness was essential. But if I was too stealthy, too aloof, or worse yet, too speedy, the object of my desire would disappear well before I arrived.

A spotting usually starts with a feeling that something's off—a limb of a tree that's a bit too dark, a peculiar shape in a bush, or a light-colored blob high up in a cavity of an oak tree.

The hole that held the light-colored blob in question was the perfect spot for an owl nest. The leaves were off the trees, but I still couldn't get a clear view through the thick stands of saplings and evergreens. All I needed for a decent photo was a sliver of a tunnel through the thin branches. I found myself inching farther and farther away.

Shifting my attention to finding a parent owl, whose presence should've been guaranteed if the light-colored blob was indeed an owlet, I examined every deformed lump on limbs and trunks. I activated my peripheral awareness. I scrutinized strange patterns in the leaves and branches, but I didn't see any owls. I closed my eyes and listened.

Once, while in the woods, I heard a strange little noise, like a puppy crying itself to sleep. The murmuring came from halfway up an old oak, where a Great Horned Owl pretended to be a lump on a limb. Its eyes were slits, as if it was half awake, half asleep. So, while I searched for an owl through the saplings, I listened for puppy sounds. The owls weren't murmuring that day though.

Eventually, I found a spot that gave me an acceptable vantage point of the cavity. It was farther away than I'd hoped, but it was the best I could do.

I'm easily fooled by strange shapes in cavities of trees. I once went crazy taking photos of what I thought was a Barn Owl, only to zoom in on the shots later to find an adorable owl-shaped pattern in the inner bark of the tree. After that, I constantly questioned what I saw.

But this time something was actually in the cavity—something round, something breathing. Raising my binoculars, I saw the fluffy, white feathers on the crown of a baby Great Horned Owl's head. From a distance, the exposed part of the head was no more than four inches across and two inches high. The second I spotted it in my binoculars, it moved, and an eye appeared over the rim of the cavity. It looked me squarely in the eyes. I froze, but I couldn't keep from giggling. Its head sank down, and the eye was gone. I tried to imagine what the nest looked like and wondered if there was a second owlet.

I raised my camera and zoomed in. The baby had moved over a little, and its beak sat neatly in a vertical slat of the tree. Two golden eyes were homed in on me. The unwavering look made my skin prickle.

It was dusk, and as the baby owl began to rouse, one of its wings flipped up into view. Then its eyelids closed and its sleepy-baby-owl body sank down into the nest again.

I'd ignored the ubiquitous crows that had congregated in a nearby tree. But the baby owl knew something was up. Breaking its connection with me, it swiveled its head in the direction of the quickly growing number of noisy, quarrelsome crows. I followed the baby's gaze and saw black wings settling on almost every branch of the neighboring trees. More crows circled overhead while others descended from the darkening sky in droves. The baby owl didn't flinch or hide when a platoon of crows careened past the nest. Its head simply turned side-to-side as if it was watching lightning bugs in its yard.

Anxiety rose in my throat, but I thought, "Crows wouldn't attack an owl. It's too big, even if it is a baby. I never heard of such a thing."

Then a thunderous noise erupted and swarms of swirling black wings, extended claws, and open beaks descended on the nest. I screamed, "NO!" But it was done—they were on the baby owl.

Suddenly, a huge creature swooped up from below. It took a second to register that it was a brown bird, the mother Great Horned Owl. She flung her body between her baby and the murder of crows. Then she enfolded it with her outstretched wings. The relentless crows hurled themselves into the mother's back, but she kept her wings up and her head down. She glanced behind her once, but never faltered.

Down below, I was in full panic mode. I had to do something. I clapped as loudly as I could. At first, nothing happened. I'm not sure the crows heard me through the pandemonium, but I kept clapping, loud—and hard—and spaced out—in order to catch their attention. A few crows glared at me. Waving my arms, I clapped and shouted until their deadly formation loosened. A group of them swooped low over my head before taking off into the encroaching dusk. Eventually, the rest of the crows seemed to realize that their backup had thinned, and they flew away across the pond to roost in a tall stand of trees.

After the last stubborn stragglers had gone, all that was left was the crows' oppressively chilling energy, which lingered in the trees like a cloud of "what almost was." My heart hammered against my chest. Tears streamed down my cheeks. I hoped the owls were okay. The mother Great Horned Owl raised her head to scan the sky, and then she spun her head around and made eye contact with me. Her gaze held me in place, and as her wide-open pupils took me in, the physical distance between us seemed to shrink. It was humbling to be acknowledged by a Great Horned Owl. Whether I actually got the crows to back off or they left on their own, I was sure she was aware that I'd tried to help. I sensed she was thanking me, or at the very least, she was acknowledging the significance of our fleeting cross-species connection.

The owlet's fluffy white head popped up and reached its face up to its mom. The mother owl bent its head down to nuzzle its baby. It was a teary reunion, at least from behind the camera. Two owl heads, one large, one tiny, swiveled to scan the trees. Then the mother kept watch while her baby cuddled up beneath her and fell asleep. As silent dusk descended (or ascended, in the world of nocturnal creatures), the mother owl clambered into the tree cavity with its lone baby and waited for true dark.

Part Two

Quechee Gorge Bridge

"Bob's gone."

"What?"

"Your brother—he's finally done it." Mom's shaky voice faded away on the last words. I imagined her arthritic hands clasping the phone to her moist cheek.

My powerless body dropped onto the couch.

It was November 2nd, 2007. I was fifty-two. It didn't take long for my brain to register that Bob had killed himself; I'd had decades of mental preparation. He'd tried it before. Once as a failed overdose in high school, and once after escaping an indentured life as a Moonie. Since then, he'd married and had three sons. There was a divorce.

Ken used to suspend a pillow over my head while the three of us watched TV. He'd hold it there until suddenly, just when I'd forgotten about it—*wham*—it would come down on my head. Hearing of Bob's death felt like that pillow had finally, once and for all, come crashing down.

Waves of sweet memories, mostly forgotten for years, came to me as snapshots: Bob smiling crookedly as he held up a fish on the line, or wearing his tiger pajamas while doing headstands on the bed. Other more involved, movie-type memories surfaced in the overnight hours—where the soft light of dawn seemed never to come.

Our cherry-red Rambler station wagon was packed with fishing tackle, games, blankets, a beach umbrella, and a cooler of sandwiches, drinks, and snacks. Scrappy's ears and tongue flapped in the wind as she sat on Bob's lap next to the window.

The short drive from our house to the Hudson River in Dobbs Ferry culminated in a curvy ride down a hill where we crossed *clickity-clack* over a wooden bridge that spanned the Hudson Line tracks. When the aroma of oil and tar hit my senses, excitement fluttered in my chest.

Dad staked out our spot in the park by plunging the beach umbrella into the grass next to a picnic table. Mom spread out the red and white checked tablecloth while we kids unloaded the car. After setting up the badminton net and horseshoes, we grabbed our fishing gear and headed for the river.

My fishing rod was short and pink—too girly for me really, but it was the right size. Besides Little Pink, I got to carry my new green and white tackle box plus the can of worms. The wet leaves in the woods behind our house provided a cornucopia of wrigglers. I loved the earthy smell of worm dirt, but I was only marginally aware of feelings of guilt as to the fate of the can's inhabitants. I hated threading those squirmy, icky things onto the hook. The tiny bits of wet dirt on their skin felt gritty between my fingers. When it came time to thread the "bait," I held my breath, gripped the hook, and touched the sharp tip to what I thought was the worm's head. Its body wriggled against my palm. Slime oozed everywhere. I thought I might cry.

"Give it here," said Bob. It just took a flip of the wrist and the hook was baited.

Our fishing spot was an outcropping of black angular rocks that ran the length of the park. Downriver to our left, I could see the George Washington Bridge and, farther away in the distance, the edges of the city itself. Directly across the river was the New Jersey Palisades, a sheer wall of rock that abutted the water like a fortress.

I knew it could take a while for anything to happen. I was having fun and secretly wished nothing *would* happen. But then there was a sharp tug at my line and I nearly dropped Little Pink. I gripped the handle with both hands. My heart thumped as if the creature on my hook was in my chest. The thing tugged and tugged, like a train jerking over bad track. Suddenly, it became a steady pull. The fish wove back and forth as Little Pink's flimsy reel spit out line, allowing the thing to pull farther away from shore. The sea creature was strong—way stronger than me. I couldn't believe that my brothers didn't notice what was happening. Their lines were slack. They stared at the sky, scratched their stomachs, and yawned.

My line swerved side to side, slicing the water like a scalpel slices skin. It pulled and tugged and jerked until my hands turned white.

"Reel it in!" Bob screamed. "Little Pink's gonna break!" I tried to crank the handle, but it wouldn't budge. I leaned back and crouched down. Bob took the rod out of my shaking hands and firmly planted his foot on a rock. The rod bent and danced spastically as he fought to reel in my river monster.

"I might have to cut the line," he said. "You need a better rod. What the hell did you catch anyway?"

He cranked and cranked until beads of sweat covered his forehead. Progress was measured in inches. When the line entered the water just in front of the rocks, he handed Little Pink back to me. He nodded and smiled. My arms were still trembling, but maybe the thing was tired too. I reeled it in the rest of the way, and eventually, its head broke through the surface of the water. Two more cranks, one swift lift of the rod, and out it came. It was the ugliest, skinniest, longest fish I'd ever seen. Water flew everywhere as the fish thrashed on the line. I didn't hesitate doing what Bob had taught me to do—I firmly grabbed the thing below the mouth and got ready to remove the hook before finally throwing it in the bucket. The instant I wrapped my fist around the creature's neck, it wound its body around my arm. Bob gasped. I didn't know what to do. Its grip was getting tighter and tighter.

"Stay right where you are. Whatever you do, don't let go!"

Bob picked up the net and then threw it down again. Searching the ground, he came back with a rock the size of a brick.

"Ready? You've got to be very brave, sis. Look away if you want."

I turned away, but I still heard the thud when the rock came down on the eel's head. My final memory of that day is of my brother's tear-stained face as he unwound the creature from my arm, cut the line, and tossed the floppy gray eel back into the Hudson.

I moved my thumb over the TV remote. The Golden Gate Bridge filled the screen. It was night, and the bridge's burnt orange shape was lit by thousands of glimmering lights. I'd inadvertently tuned in to a special on bridges and the people who jump from them. My heart pounded as my finger flinched over the channel button. Stumbling upon footage of people plummeting into San Francisco Bay made my throat constrict. My body went limp.

I'd been over the Golden Gate a couple of times, and was lucky once to see a golden eagle soaring past.

Vigilantly surveying the bridge for potential jumpers, there were security cameras and rescue crews standing by 24-7. The suicide attempts were mostly successful, but many were thwarted by dangerous rescues or guards who talked people back over to the safe side of the protective railings. There was an interview with one jumper who managed to survive as a paraplegic. He regretted the attempt to take his own life, but not because of his injuries. His rescue led to a better life than he'd ever envisioned—a life he'd almost missed.

The 4 train at Bowling Green left the station like a pellet from a slingshot. Careening through the tunnels, we belly laughed as we tumbled and slid on the sideways seats. Sparks revealed the shocking closeness of the tunnel's walls, but every few minutes, the train screamed past a blur of brightly lit activity at the stations, which lasted only as long as the flash of a camera. The express never slowed, and as the train jolted and screeched its way uptown, it seemed likely that we'd jump the tracks at the next curve or eventually the flickering lights would go off permanently and we'd be stranded in a dark underworld to be devoured by rabid rats or subway bats. So long as we kept moving, there was nothing to fear.

We'd spent a day in lower Manhattan at Battery Park, where we rode the Staten Island Ferry, which cost five cents each way, and then boarded the subway back to Grand Central, where we'd catch the Hudson Line home. That morning, Mom dropped us off at the train in Dobbs Ferry, and at the end of the day, Dad met us downtown where he escorted us to the subway stop. We were used to it. It was fun.

The train's windows were all the way down, but it was still stifling down there below the city. Bob had bought a balloon for me in the subway station—one of those bulging blimps about six feet long and a foot wide. Swirly White was the best balloon ever. Because it needed lots of room, it sat/hovered next to me on the bench seat.

At one point, I tapped the balloon across the aisle. Bob tapped it back. Despite the jostling ride and raging wind in the tunnels, we successfully hit it across the aisle dozens of times. Opening the white paper bags of candy we'd bought from a street vendor, we snacked on Orange Circus Marshmallow Peanuts, Atomic Fireballs, and Wax Bottles—all while keeping the balloon aloft. We were a giggling, candy-munching, balloon-bumping machine.

Then, without warning, Ken punched the balloon and it zoomed up to the ceiling, where it hovered under the flickering lights like a nightmare version of the Dumbo balloon in The Macy Thanksgiving Day Parade. Then Swirly White got sucked out the window at cartoon speed, shimmying between the train and the tunnel wall before zipping out of sight.

Tears welled up in my eyes. Bob's jaw dropped as he glared at our brother. Then the two of them broke down laughing. It *was* funny. The balloon rocketing out the window was so unexpected, so preposterous. It was a ghost being sucked into the netherworld—gone in a split second.

The overnight hours stretched out mercilessly. I was fidgety. I'm not an I'm-upset-so-what-can-I-clean? sort of person. Still, I grabbed a dust rag and sat at my desk. I opened the top right drawer. Sitting on a stack of papers was a notecard from Bob. Could I bring myself to touch it—now that he'd died? I wasn't ready for a message from the newly dead. Dropping the rag, I watched my hand reach out and pick up the card.

The picture on the front was hand-drawn: an arching footbridge over a babbling brook. The water's edge was bordered with delicate wildflowers. A card from my brother was rare, but I couldn't remember when I'd gotten it.

It had been difficult for Bob to accept my lesbianism. My "lifestyle" wasn't something I considered newsworthy, so I never felt the need to officially "come out." Bob asked about it once though, and after I confirmed it, he said, "So . . . it was just that one time, right? I mean, if you meet someone that you really like, and even if she's really cute, you wouldn't do it again, would you?" "Uh, yeah, Bob. I would."

I was in my twenties then, and being gay was simply who I was. But was I delusional for thinking that having a lesbian sister would automatically feel normal to my brother? Over time, a chasm had grown in the space where my words—and his words—should've been.

I ran my fingertips across the drawing on Bob's note. His tiny scrawl was intimate, as if it contained secrets. I wasn't ready for the heartfelt message I found inside, but I couldn't stop reading. He was glad I'd found love and a place to call home. He sounded like the brother I'd adored so profoundly as a child. How had I let him slip away?

Part Three

Christmas in the Bronx

Every year when I was a kid, somewhere between Thanksgiving and Christmas, my family would visit the Billoses, my mother's sister's family. Their detached row house contributed to the neighborhood's insane Christmas light display, which created an aura-like glow seen from blocks away. When we turned onto their street, it looked more like Main Street, North Pole, than a blue-collar neighborhood in the Bronx. It didn't matter that the street hadn't been plowed or that the trash hadn't been picked up. It didn't matter that it was nighttime. The outrageously luminescent homes must've been empty inside because entire extended families of Italians, Puerto Ricans, and Ukrainians were outside laughing, drinking, and shooting craps by a wall on a cleared-off section of sidewalk. Across the street from my cousins', a group of guys was singing, "Shake it, marimba, shake it . . . shake it as hard as you can!"

Even though I was escorted by my father, two brothers, and my mother, at least one of the guys always had a lewd remark for me. "Hey, little girl, want a drink?" "Don't go with them. We're a lot more fun." I knew it was their version of joking around, but I averted my eyes just in case.

Christmas lights outlined every contour of the Billos's house and bushes, plus, special red strands twirled around the railings that led to the tinsel-covered, red-bowed front door. Bells tinkled when the door opened. Aunt Helen and my three cousins, Tommy, Andrew, and Mark greeted us with awkward one-armed hugs and gawky smiles. Uncle Johnny waved to us from his Archie Bunker-type chair that sat next to a modestly decorated tree. There weren't any small stuffed animals hanging from the branches. It was mostly shiny balls, strands of beads, and a few Ukrainian ornaments my grandmother brought with her from the homeland when she was a child.

The party in the streets raged on, but inside, there was nothing to do. Tommy, the eldest, sat with his knees glued together while he wrung his hands and smiled in confused non-participation. I thought he was sweet, and when we made eye contact, he mumbled a few words and I smiled back. After dinner, Andrew and Mark watched football with Uncle Johnny. Dad fell asleep reading the *New York Post* while my mother and Aunt Helen shared afghan patterns and packed up leftovers.

The house was decorated in shades of brown, but scattered around on the tables, walls, and couches were items made by my grandmother: colorful embroideries of Russian farmers in front of fancy onion-topped orthodox churches, hand-stitched pillow covers, and piles of afghans.

The bathroom was pink. Towels, plush rugs, plush toilet seat cover, bouncy plastic toilet seat, flamingo toilet brush, shower curtain, soap, woven laundry basket, and textured wallpaper—all pink. The tile in the tub was lime green. I wanted to take off my socks and let the soft fibers of the rug squish between my toes, but the overpowering smell of rose made my throat sting and my eyes water.

The street was deserted by the time we left. As we walked to the car, I glanced behind me to see my boot prints on the fresh dusting of snow that obscured the craps patch on the sidewalk. Fog had transformed the street into a cozy valley of blurry, multi-colored halos, and as the headlights of our silver, tail-finned Impala swung around in the red-tinged air, I rested my cheek on the cool window and closed my eyes.

Prune Danish

Pavement, buildings, sidewalks, sky: all was gray. Even the scrawny trees, dying of thirst in their small squares of gravel, were gray. I clung to my father's hand as we passed through the unmanned, unlocked "security gates" and down urine-infested hallways to the thick metal door of my maternal grandparents' apartment. The projects in the Bronx were a scary place.

When the door swung open, we were greeted by my rotund grandmother and bone-skinny grandfather, who uttered a Ukrainian phrase I knew well, translated as, "Give me a kiss on the lips." Grandpa didn't speak much English, but he didn't need to. Despite yellowed and missing teeth, his wide smile revealed love. His breath smelled like prune danish and coffee. Grandpa breath.

Before I knew it, I was gobbled up into Grandma's generous bosom. "My sweet Carol," she said. She wore a babushka and clothes made of colorful fabric. I tugged on the embroidered hanky peeking out from her sleeve. She smothered me with kisses.

Their tiny apartment was always stuffy, but the savory aromas of Ukrainian food cooking in the kitchen made it feel homey and safe. Their closet and bedroom doors had been switched out for heavy drapery—a quirky but cozy setup that solved the problem of swinging doors in a tight space. My grandparents were all wrinkles, warm hands, and smiles. They slurped their coffee, which was filled to the brim and loaded up with three generous teaspoons of sugar each. Four danishes—two cheese and two prune—were cut into eight pieces. Plenty for all of us, plus one extra.

The table in the dual-purpose dining/living room was always set for the next meal. At Thanksgiving, Ukrainian bowls were heaped with pierogies, kielbasa, holubtsi, kapusta, ham, turkey, yams, green beans, babka, and borscht. Mom brought the pies, but my grandparents made the rest, and I tried to fit some of everything on my plate, except for the bitter borscht and mysterious mincemeat pie. In the summers, my grandparents were cooks at a Ukrainian camp in the Catskills, so everything in their narrow kitchen was oversized: serving utensils, pots, lids, ladles, and of course—cookie jars.

They'd never encountered any crime in the projects until, one day, Grandma returned from the store and noticed a sheet dangling from their apartment window. She found Grandpa slumped over in his chair. He was bound and gagged, and a knife was plunged into his chest. The coffee can where they kept a handful of coins lay empty on the table.

Three Men in Black: Icons of Spirituality

After my grandfather's funeral, dreams came to me draped in gauze. Sometimes, my eyes searched the insides of my eyelids for movement or shape—anything symbolizing the tangible. Often, a dream would begin with just a voice. Imagery came after.

ஓ

"Moonlit snow blanketed the ground. Stars bejeweled the vast night sky."

Six globes of yellow light floated in space. My equilibrium was off kilter and brain fluid sloshed around in my skull. I expanded and contracted my lungs, and suddenly, three Victorian carriages appeared, each with two yellow lanterns affixed to the front end. Black fabric covered the windows, but I knew there were caskets inside. The relics were parked in front of my house. I wondered how they'd had enough power to get up the hill.

Three men in black stood by their respective carriages—ready to receive me, should I choose. The man by the first carriage looked exactly like the depiction of Jesus that hung in my grandparents' apartment. But in my dream version, Jesus had darker skin. His hand was raised in a gesture of blessing. His lips were neutral, but his eyes smiled with anticipation.

The second man was shorter than Jesus by almost a foot. I liked and feared him all at once. His charcoal black, curly hair and bushy eyebrows formed a single tsunami over his glimmering black eyes. A neatly trimmed, dark-as-licorice beard and dense mustache circumvented his cheeks, which were round and glossy with sweat. When he grinned, his substantial blood-red lips blemished the sepia and black color palette of my dream.

The third man's face was hidden behind an opaque black veil. His beard hung down below the veil like Spanish moss clinging to an ancient oak. The man held a bouquet of ivory roses. They were not for me. They were for Grandpa.

Uncle Peter

There was ample room on Uncle Peter's massive lap to nestle in his generous arms while he strummed his ukulele and sang, "When I was a little bitty baby, my momma used to rock me in the cradle . . ." He smelled of garlic, gin, Brylcreem, and a repulsive mix of urine and whatever antiseptic product comprised the contents of the bag tucked behind the back of his wheelchair. The smile on his cherub-like, dimpled face was as sweet and effortless as an infant's.

Lore had it that when he was a young man he was shot by his lover's enraged husband. "It was a case of mistaken identity," my mother told me.

Sometimes, Uncle Peter showed up at our house driving his hand-operated silver Datsun 240z. Other times, he drove a baby blue station wagon packed with a trove of children who were possibly, or possibly not, my biological cousins. He had two wives, one of whom was not actually married to him.

Before he moved to Hawaii, we had a rare gathering at our house. My grandparents were there, as well as the Billoses. When it was time to say goodbye, Uncle Peter executed an impressively smooth routine of maneuvering himself into the driver's seat, single-handedly hoisting the chair into the back of his sports car, and lifting his legs into the hollow space beneath the dash. He drew me in against his chest and burrowed my face into his soft neck. "Be good, Carol girl," he whispered.

My throat constricted as I looked up at the unfailingly taciturn faces of my parents, brothers, and cousins. The brightest star in my family's night sky was leaving our galaxy. How could they just stand there? Then, as the car pulled away, I heard Grandpa whimper. He reached into the air. "Petee, Petee!" he cried. His trembling voice was so startling, so compelling—I wanted more than anything to be alone with his precious display of love.

The Pilgrimage

I tried to imagine what my grandparents must've felt as their little fists grasped the rail on deck of the *Wilhelm II*—straining to keep sight of their respective parents on shore as they grew smaller and smaller, until all that was left was ocean stretching out in all directions. I wish I knew what their mother and father had said to them as they dressed little Thomas and little Anastasia in their warmest clothing for a one-way journey across the ocean. How did they decide which photos, toys, and heirlooms to stuff in their suitcases?

Fifty years after being processed through Ellis Island with her new friend and future husband, Thomas Kuzil, my widowed grandmother, whose friends knew her as "Hope," went back to Ukraine to visit the village of her birth. Wiping her lips between sips of coffee, she told me how she placed flowers on her parents' graves and revisited her childhood home. She unpacked the suitcase she'd stuffed with blue jeans and nylons from America, which she gave to great-nephews and nieces she never knew existed until then. She reunited with the only surviving member of her immediate family, an older brother who she hadn't seen since the day she boarded that ship. Her chin quivered when she told me that they recognized each other right away—after all that time.

Part Four

Heritage

My relationship with the piano department at The Hartt School of Music began at my audition, which foreshadowed things to come, including shenanigans from Ray Hanson, my teacher's husband and the department head. He came running into the studio fifteen minutes late, panting and hugging a football under his arm. "Wait for me, did you, little shmuggums?" He tapped the top of my head with his fingers, then hopped up, tippy-toed, onto the available two inches behind my butt on the piano bench.

"Oh, Rayski," said Miss Koscielny. "Let the girl play. Go on, Carol, dear."

My relationship with my piano teacher, Anne Koscielny, began with the *Appassionata* Sonata by Beethoven, *Carnaval* by Schumann, and the 24 Preludes Op. 11 by Scriabin. Her markings in my scores are treasures to me now; and when, in the course of my own teaching, I stumble upon one of her jewels, I share the significance of my find with my students. In addition to the sound musical advice and fingerings she inserted among the composers' markings, "clearer here please, less left hand, continue to listen, Carol . . . even though it happens to be *forte!,*" her elegant handwriting has a meaning of its own. It reveals that an invested, generous teacher was there. Her spirit was big-hearted and noncompetitive, and she regularly assigned pieces for which she herself was known: Ravel's *Gaspard de la Nuit,* the Barber Sonata, the Chopin Concertos, Beethoven's 32 Sonatas.

Later, I would encourage my students to play "my" repertoire too. Why not be generous? The point wasn't to duplicate my touch, nuance, and interpretation. If they were expert imitators—which many were—they'd have to figure out their own style eventually, or I'd help them find it.

Collaborative skills gleaned from my formative years of playing four-hand music with Dad gave me an instant "in" with singers and instrumentalists. I experienced a musician's version of being popular in high school. As a fluent sight-reader, I learned reams of music quickly. It was second nature for me to listen primarily to a vocalist or violinist while simultaneously balancing and voicing my own part. I focused on consonants at the inception of words in sung text, and I carefully timed my part to sound with the ensuing vowel in order to create pleasingly accurate ensemble. I listened for changes in pressure and speed of a string player's bow, or the support and flow of air beneath a wind player's or singer's tone—all indicators of rubato and nuance.

Playing vocal recitals and chamber music allowed me to stretch my collaborative muscle, which benefitted my solo playing. The thread of energy that sustains a phrase is powered by motion and intention. Given the inherent flaws of our instrument, pianists perpetually seek seamless legato and smooth, gradual dynamics. Pianos have a thing called natural diminution, or decay, wherein tone begins to dissipate soon after a key is depressed. String players, wind players, vocalists, and organists have the ability to sustain and even crescendo on a single note. Pianists can't actually do this, but with the proper technical and listening skills, we can make it seem as if we can. The influence of vocalists and instrumentalists is a powerful thing.

While at Hartt, I performed dozens of collaborative recitals and eight solo recitals, four of which had repertoire chosen by Miss Koscielny and me, and four comprised of repertoire assigned to me as part of the annual study project of a featured composer's *oeuvre*. The summer before my freshman year, I received a note from the piano department listing which four Beethoven Sonatas I was to prepare. I'd found my people.

I became fluent in solfege, the use of *do-re-mi-fa-sol-la-ti-do,* which was taught by an impassioned, perpetually energized woman. She cursed in Hungarian every time a student pronounced *sol* as *so.* I discovered a love for the system of moveable *do,* where *do* represents the tonic, or root, of a key. The syllables have musical need or resolution. *Sol* craves *do,* as does *ti.* Try singing the scale using *do-re-mi,* and stop on *ti.* You'll see what I mean. *Do* can be any note in the scale, and migrates as harmonies modulate. When I got to Juilliard, I learned fixed *do,* where *do* is always C. I rebelled against the meaningless use of the musically inclined syllables. Except for atonal music, which lacks tonal center, fixed *do* renders music heartless.

Since I'd entered freshman studies at the third-year level, my actual junior year included a "philosophy class" that masqueraded as Music Theory VII. We read fragments from Arthur Schopenhauer's *The World as Will and Representation,* and *The Art of Being Right,* and we discussed the philosophy of using artistic and moral awareness to overcome the human condition of pain and conflict.

Carol Rich

The Glowing Fugue

Bach's Fugue in A Minor from Book I of the *Well-Tempered Clavier* is a massive four-part fugue, one of the longest and most demanding. It was past midnight, and hours of memory work on the fugue had tied my brain in knots. My fingers were winding their way around a particularly tricky passage when there was a knock at the door. It wasn't unusual for one of the other obsessed pianists to take a break and say hi. I removed my piano glasses and rubbed my eyes.

When I opened the door, my friend Melvin was standing there with a thin, wide grin on his face. He was an imposing guy: tall, slim, with a blond goatee that seemed to be hidden by day and visible by night. He wore his usual, slightly odorous, black clothes, and was known as a lovable lurker, an eccentric.

He drove a hearse, which had the name HEATH etched into the long window beside where a casket would sit. I always read the H as a D, until I remembered it was just Melvin's car. I'd gone out-and-about with him several times, but I never got used to the slightly suspect aroma inside, or the nagging impulse to check over my shoulder.

Lore had it that Melvin spent his nights resting atop an upright in the cells, the cement-walled practice rooms in the far reaches of the basement used mainly by non-piano majors.

Raising his eyebrows, Melvin held out several pages of manuscript paper. "A gift for you," he said. He bowed, flipped off the lights, and backed out of the room.

I was holding a copy of the A Minor Fugue—hand written in phosphorescent green ink. Even the lines of the staff were hand drawn. It was still moist, and the writing was so dense, I suspected it might never dry. The paper sagged from the weight of it. Writing out four measures in such globby ink would've been impressive. This was, well . . . insane.

Leaving the lights off, I put the music on the piano rack and started to play, but the score wasn't easy to read. The blotchy ink made it hard to decipher on which lines the note-heads fell. I shook my head. I was too frazzled to mess with it. Plus, Melvin's gesture of friendship, as amazing as it was, had a strong creep factor. I packed up for the night.

It was near 2 A.M. by the time I finally got under the sheets. I relaxed my mind and listened to the cricket that had moved in somewhere in my bedroom. I thought about the solid memory work I'd done on the fugue and prepared my mind for the next day's lesson.

Suddenly, I saw Melvin's pale face appear outside my second-story bedroom window. No doubt he'd climbed a tree, but he insisted that he'd floated up there. I don't remember how I got rid of him, but it was quick. One day, he disappeared for good.

Carol Rich

The Lib

The Datsun's turn signal played crazy syncopations against the smooth jazz riff of the raggedy windshield wipers, *click-a-whish-click-a-dipadoooo-click-a-whish*. . . . But inside my head, the incessantly repetitive sixteenth-note pattern of *Paganini,* from Schumann's *Carnaval,* buzzed around like trapped bees. An hour had passed since I'd left the practice room, but my hands on the steering wheel still twitched with perpetual motion staccato octaves. The car's ambient rhythms jived with the goings-on in my head.

I'd been warned about venturing downtown into Hartford's sepia, nighttime gloom—not because of crime, but on account of its after-sundown aura of oppressiveness. I kept my head down and lowered the volume on my inter-cranial madness. My hands relaxed on the steering wheel.

Just past the city limits, I turned onto an apartment-lined brick street where amber light reflected in gutter puddles. I half expected to see a young Marlon Brando lurking in a doorway—his face is spot-lit as a match's sudden flash meets the tip of his cigarette.

A blurry glow of red neon revealed the location of my destination. I inched the car forward until, between windshield wiper swipes, I made out the luminous words, "The Lib." Then, as if giving a secret signal, the sign blinked once before returning to perfunctory on-ness. I eyeballed the recessed doorway beside the sign and pulled into a spot out front. I cut the engine, and lifting the collar on my leather jacket, I stepped out into the drizzle and made a dash for it.

The initial stink of stale cigarettes and beer stirred an appealingly sweet, yet seedy creature in my chest. The door thudded shut behind me, and I scanned the dozen or so curious faces that turned in my direction. The creature cooed and hummed.

The ceiling—from the door, the bar, booths, dance floor, candlelit tables, pool table, and all the way back to a mysteriously curtained doorway—was festooned with white lights. Behind the bar, shelves of colorful booze bottles were backlit in blue light. A tattered poster of Kate Jackson hung over the tall-backed, red-cushioned booths across from the bar.

"Well, hello there, sweetcakes!" The husky voice emanated from one of the booths. "Where'd you wander in from?" The woman's bloodshot eyes tried to focus on me. She sat across from a leather-vested, gray-haired woman. "Come sit with us, honey," she said. She scooched over, closer to the wall.

"Uh . . . thanks. I'm just looking around."

"Aren't we all? Let us by you a drink, sugar."

"Thanks anyway, maybe next time."

I sat at the bar, two stools down from a lanky woman who nodded and glanced past the curtain of her long black hair to flick a tight smile in my direction. She ran her index finger around the rim of her drink.

Wiping at the already-clean spot in front of me, the bartender said, "I'm Kim. What can I get you?"

"Just decaf, thanks. Black."

Kim was big-boned, heavily eye-shadowed, and slightly whiskered.

"No problem. Here you go, kid."

"Thanks."

The small, female-shaped mug had the perfect curvature for my hand. Tossing some cash on the bar, I went to sit by the pool table. I put my name on the chalkboard and watched two women hack away at the cue ball as if they were trying to shoot a dead fly off the red felt. Across the table in a dark corner by the ladies' room, I noticed someone glaring at me from beneath her generous eyebrows. I nodded, but she looked away and leaned in to her friend who glanced at me and chuckled.

The cue ball flew past its target and slammed—*thud*—into the corner pocket.

"I'm up next," said a gravelly voice. It was the glaring woman. She swaggered toward the table like a lazy bull going to assess its cows coming over the rise. She erased the only two names on the board: Lou and Carol. Then she motioned to me. "Let's go. Yer up."

The rules were clearly posted: winner plays the next person on the list.

"It's okay. I can wait," I said.

Lou snarled at the woman who won by default. "You don't mind, do you, Cat?"

"Nah. Go for it." Cat returned her stick to the rack and then grabbed the hand of her date. Hands on each other's knee, they sat at the table next to mine.

I'd been loyal to my six-hour practice day routine, but my breaks, which seemed to be getting longer and longer, were spent shooting pool in the student union building across the quad from the music building. I'd recently placed second in a women's pool tournament, so my reservoir of confidence was still intact. Sure, I'd been utterly creamed and humiliated in the final round, but how was I expected to focus when my opponent was a Kate Jackson lookalike? I glanced at the poster and felt my competitive blood roil.

Lou's thick thumbs flipped up the clasps on her pool stick box. She twisted together the segments of the custom-made stick, twirled the tip in a cube of blue chalk, powdered her hands, clapped clouds of white into the air, and then racked up the balls. After tamping each one down with the cue ball, she gingerly lifted the rack. It's a rude racking technique, designed to make the break hard to scatter for the likes of me—someone who'd never lifted weights in her life and who'd been building finger strength instead of brawn.

After evaluating the selection of The Lib's pool sticks, I chose a nearly straight, nicely weighted one. I could work with it.

"Don't let her win." Engrossed in finding the best stick, I didn't notice the waitress passing by. When she whispered in my ear, the sensation of our hair intermingling gave me chills. "Name's Gail. I'll see *you* later." She exuded an exotically earthy aroma as she grazed up against me before placing two tall, frosted glasses of beer in front of Cat and date.

"Your break . . . tootsie." Blowing blue dust off of the tip of her stick, Lou smirked as if she'd already won.

I dabbed at the chalk and rubbed blue between my first and second knuckles where I would slide the cue stick. My unique bridge technique—thumb, fourth, and fifth fingertips on the felt, second and third fingers curled above the table—made my hand feel like a raptor's claw.

I aimed the cue ball to strike the corner ball of the rack, where another ball would escape from the pack, bank against the cushion at the foot of the table, and travel straight back past the pack and into the corner pocket to my right. After finessing the shot, I employed a psychological device Kate Jackson had used on me—I avoided eye contact with Lou. I kept my gaze on the table. The remaining balls had separated just enough to pick off the next four shots, but even though the first shot was the hardest, I missed one of the easy ones.

Lou sauntered around the table and made six shots in a row. I sipped my decaf and scanned the room. Five names had been added to the pool list, and it seemed like everyone in the place had congregated around the table. Lou rushed an easy shot. "Damn it," she mumbled. After nicking one of my balls, the cue ball had rolled to a stop behind her last ball and the eight ball. It left me without a direct path to my balls. She smirked again.

"The fancier the better," I mumbled. I jumped the cue ball and made my shot. The path to a win was in my sights. I executed a basic bank shot followed by a sharply angled, gentle kiss to the eight ball that fell like an exclamation point into the side pocket.

"Again," said Lou. She quickly re-racked.

"Uh, no thanks. You can play the next person."

"Uh, no. Your break."

I returned my stick to the wall rack and downed the dregs in the bottom of my mug. "No thanks."

Suddenly, Lou lunged in front of me. "You cheated," she said. Her breath reeked of onions and beer.

"What? How . . . ?"

"Are you calling *me* a cheater now?" she shouted.

"That doesn't even make sense," I said.

Lou's red-faced friend jumped to her side.

Then, Kim and Gail quickly situated themselves between Lou and me. Kim, who was a foot taller than Lou, said, "Cool down, my friend. Come on, Carol . . . I could use some help behind the bar."

Gail reached back, found my hand, and then threaded her cool fingers with mine. My pulse raced wildly.

I became a regular at the The Lib. I sat at the bar and had beers with the lanky, long-haired woman who turned out to be the most popular lesbian in the community, and the most dance-addicted person I'd ever known. I schmoozed in the booth with the two older dykes, Patsy and Pam, as they good-naturedly harassed the new blood that wandered in. I discovered what hid behind the curtain in the back: a graffiti-spattered, smells-like-car-freshener bathroom that was locked from the inside most of the time. I even shot pool with Lou's friend Marge, whose red face was actually caused by rosacea, not anger. But, I admit that I flinched whenever I saw Lou's sawn-off-car El Camino sitting out front.

Gail and I became friends/almost lovers—a common designation given to most of my lesbian relationships in those days. Hers was one of the apartments on the same street as The Lib. It always smelled of a confusing blend of cinnamon and kitty litter.

One night, as we sipped beer from her ever-ready frosted glasses, I swooned from the intoxicating aroma of her hair. She wept while she laid bare stories about her recent breakup with Cat, who purposefully flaunted her dates at The Lib.

Late one night that same week, after playing several rounds of pool, I found myself standing on the street looking up at Gail's window. As usual, the curtains were backlit by the small table lamp, which sat next to a temperamental, hissing radiator. Gail hadn't been to The Lib all week and my craving for her scent pulled me forward. I took a few stealthy strides toward her apartment. Just then, someone drew the curtains open. I froze. A woman's silhouette appeared in the window, and then the light went out. I never returned to that street again.

Carol Rich

Mumblings

Sweat poured down my back. John, the only man I'd ever spend a night with—albeit a sexless one—kept his apartment at sauna temperature. The windows had been flung open, but it was a moot gesture. The promise of air was thwarted by the radiator's impermeable wall of heat that settled in front of the opening. The pores on my skin were millions of tiny mouths gasping for air. I grabbed my things and fled past the frenzied, pot-induced blur of my friends' faces.

All of a sudden, I was outside! The cool autumnal air made me moan. Tying my sweater around my waist, I rolled up my sleeves. My flight from the apartment had propelled me on, what felt like, a predestined path, one that crossed the center of the university's expansive quad. Moon glow settled on trees, buildings, and skin. I was admiring the silken quality of my arm, when I heard the familiar *scree-scree-scree* of bats echo-locating down by the Hog River. A breeze lifted the dappled leaves around my ankles, and eddies churned up all around my legs. With each new mini-tornado, the leaves' mumblings grew. I knew what they were saying. I was receiving a shadow-message from the past.

Dropping to the ground, I rolled onto my back and watched lacy black clouds slide in front of the full moon. Suddenly, I was yanked back to a parallel moment in my life when I was given a similar, more sinister message from The Beyond.

Barber's *Adagio for Strings* was resounding through the house. It was 1972, and I was at a party with high school friends. I'd consumed Cold Duck, a whisky sour, and a Molson. My stomach churned. By 3 A.M., with everyone passed out in the bedrooms or on the bathroom tile floor, my lone companion was the flickering, hissing, disapproving fireplace in the living room.

Flinging open the sliding doors to the backyard, I stepped out into a soothing mist. I threw out my arms to meet the coolness when suddenly the grass came up to meet me and I landed flat on my back. The slanting ground undulated until I steadied my gaze on a single spot in the thick cloud cover. Tears slid into my ears. I wished for morning. I wished for rain—a baptismal deluge. Then the spot overhead became an opening in the clouds, about the size of a dime. All at once, the opening expanded like the light-seeking aperture of a lens. Stars twinkled in the opening, and I saw the silhouette of my shaking hand reach up to the sky. I collapsed in on myself and sobbed.

"You will never do this again. Don't waste your life!"

It was the booming voice of God.

The leaves' mumblings were a reminder, an echo message. Yet, my euphoria was still at its peak. I leapt up and went to find the sweet spot in the middle of the quad, where I sent a series of claps resonating off the buildings. A second later, a plethora of claps zinged past me. I played with the echolalia by creating overlapping effects and dynamic changes. I intoned "echolalia" over and over. "Echolalia. Echolalia. Echolalia!" The word was unique; it didn't lose meaning with repetition. My hands tingled. Then they itched. They wanted to play.

ல

The music building should've been locked by the time I got there, but the back door was open. I went to room 131 and sat down at the dilapidated Steinway. It was a beater, a P. S. O.—a Piano Shaped

Object. A hint of cigarette smoke lingered in the air. I touched the darkened, indented piece of wood at the upper end of the keyboard where countless people had used it as an ashtray. I knew John was one of those people. I cringed at the thought, yet, the disfigurement added to the piano's charm. Its bowed, chipped plastic keys and the rough condition of the case connected me with my "student-ness." The piano was one of my people.

Holding my hands over the keys, I launched into the *Toccata* from Ravel's *Le Tombeau de Couperin.* It's a bear to play, but it was my best run-through yet. Then I noticed that something weird was going on with my eyes. The keys shimmied like eighty-eight bobbleheads whenever my hands jumped to different registers on the keyboard, which in that piece was every three seconds. Reaching up to the bridge of my nose to adjust my glasses, I realized that I was glasses-less. I must've left them at the party. I can't negotiate walking across a room without them, and I wondered how I'd made it through the labyrinth of stairs, streets, campus paths, and halls of the music building to room 131, where I'd played the entire *Toccata.* Reality shifted. Was it a phenomenal performance? Or was it shit-awful?

Beethoven

A first run-through on stage is a magical moment in the preparation of a piece, and I was eager to play through Beethoven's *Appassionata* Sonata at full tilt. It was after 11 P.M., and the main hall where my Beethoven Sonata recital was to take place was locked. I decided to play my run-through in a smaller hall, near room 131 and the cells.

The last time I performed in the hall was for a marathon event of a twenty-four hour piece called *Vexations,* by Satie. The piece consists of a one-line theme followed by a single variation to be repeated nonstop for twenty-four hours. Pianists take turns playing in two-hour shifts, seamlessly stepping in—hand-over-hand style—for the player before them. I'd signed up for two, two-hour slots. The theater seats had been temporarily removed, allowing the audience to "move in" with sleeping bags, blankets, folding chairs, and coolers of food. On occasion, students would step outside for a few minutes and reenter in a cloud of iffy smoke, the welcome residue of which wafted into the nasal passages of the performers. Even though the experience wasn't paranormal, it was fringe.

Given my high level of *Appassionata* run-through anticipation, I was relieved to find the stage door to the smaller hall unlocked. Flipping on the lights, I tossed my coat and music onto the floor. Pianists love to drop their stuff, especially coats and sweaters, next to the piano bench. Don't ask me why; from what I understand, the phenomenon is worldwide.

The seats in the hall were like movie theater seats, plush red ones of the flip-up variety, and they were empty. The 7-foot Steinway on stage was propped open at full stick. Few things in life are as stirring as being in an empty hall that's waiting to be filled with music. Even as a child, a happy thrill would pass through me before performing to a full living room of my stuffed animals.

I adjusted the piano bench that one of the taller pianists had left in the lowest position. I ran through a few scales, and then, after letting the sound fully die away, I placed my hands over the low F Minor arpeggio that begins the *Appassionata*. The moody first movement is defined by Beethoven-esque thickly voiced outbursts and an eerie four-note theme that could denote some poor soul in the grave knocking on their coffin. *Knock, knock, knock, knock.* Yes, Beethoven's Fifth Symphony might come to mind.

I'd just plunged into the thunderous development section when I heard a noise. My hands sprang off the keys. I spun around and saw a stocky man sitting behind me in the end seat of the first row. He scowled and tapped two pudgy fingers on the armrest. *Knock, knock, knock, knock.* His head was angled down, as if in judgment. He wore black slacks, a baggy off-white shirt, and a red vest closed with gold buttons. His legs were crossed, and his shoes were smudged with dirt.

I glanced down at my Beethoven Sonatas on the floor, and when I looked up, he was gone.

Tensile Strength

"Carol, you have no business playing this piece, let alone calling yourself a pianist."

The chamber music coach's bushy-eyebrowed glare sliced right through me. Gripping the edges of the piano bench, I swallowed against the lump in my throat. I knew that the speedy left-hand staccato triplet technique in the Beethoven piano trio was slightly beyond my reach, and had I been given another week, it wouldn't have been a problem. As it was, my left hand articulation was sloppy. The shock of the professor's recklessly malicious comment instantly devastated the lush musical landscape in my heart, so lovingly cultivated over time by my teachers and my father.

Muttering apologies to the violinist and cellist, I grabbed my score and ran teary-eyed from the rehearsal studio. As I leaned against the wall in the hallway, gut-deep sobs seized my body. I couldn't breathe. The one thing that defined me had been ripped from my core.

Avoiding the midday swarm of students on campus, I fled the music building through the back door, stopped on a small cement slab, wiped my eyes on my sleeve, and surveyed the undeveloped land in front of me. I'd been on the pathless route to the dorms once before, but this would be the first time on my own. I had no idea which way to go, but I did remember having started out by going downhill. Clutching my Beethoven Trios, which once belonged to Birdie, I dropped down into a ravine and snaked through the vestiges of a forsaken apple grove, half-fallen trees, and impenetrable brush. Soon, I saw the sprawling, gnarly oak that marked the spot where a wooden footbridge spanned the Hog River. I slunk past the birches and aspens where the bats roosted, and finally stumbled upon the narrow trail leading out of the ravine and up to the dorms.

Then I wept. Sitting cross-legged on my bed, I purged myself of fistfuls of shame and self-doubt—emotional states of which I was sorely unaccustomed and wholly unfit to process.

My roommate, who witnessed my breakdown from the perch of her upper bunk, jumped down, firmly took me by the arm, and led me out of the building and into her car. Ten minutes later, we were standing by a little brook in the woods.

"Listen," she said.

My sobs kept coming in fits and starts until I let in the open-throated song of the breeze in the trees and the brook's soft gurgle. The swirling memory of my botched left-hand triplets vanished. Tears spilled from my eyes and I felt my hands unclench. For the first time in my adult life, I consciously felt the tug on the gossamer-like thread that tethers nature to music—and to my soul. I learned that listening reaches deeper than merely hearing.

The Beacon

Vivid blue sky, slight breeze, chirping birds, chill in the air. It was the perfect autumn day in New England. Foliage was at its peak. Pulling on my Irish knit sweater, I packed a bag with lunch, a thermos of coffee, hat, gloves, and a copy of Adrienne Rich's *The Dream of a Common Language*. The goal was to stay outdoors until dusk. Practice guilt usually shortened the life of my self-imposed days off, and I'd find myself at the piano or in the listening lab instead of recharging away from music.

I turned the key in the ignition of my blueberry blue Datsun and the happy *chug-chug* of the engine was quickly followed by a melodious *purr*. I threw it into first and rolled away from the gravel driveway. My outings often brought on heart-pounding worry. But if my mutinous arms didn't turn the car around, eventually, stillness would come.

That day, adrenalin flooded my system the instant the tires hit pavement. The car was pointed away from campus, toward the foothills. I had a gulp of coffee. As Little Blue hummed along through winding corridors of red and gold, the rearview mirror revealed cheery eddies that swirled up in my wake. I had another sip of coffee, donned my hat, rolled down the window, and inhaled the intoxicating aroma of wood-smoke and pine. Soon, I was deep in the forest where a living wall of conifers and birches grew right up to the edge of the road. On the straightaways, a wedge of vibrant blue sky was buttressed by an open-topped tree tunnel.

After I negotiated a series of gentle S-curves, a clearing appeared through the trees, and I spotted a hand-hewn sign with the word "Abbey" on it. I was scarcely past the hidden driveway when the tree tunnel engulfed me again. Despite a momentary easing on the gas, I kept going. But I couldn't quit thinking about it. Making a U-turn on the next straightaway, I forced my headstrong foot to ease off the pedal way before the turnoff. A huge hemlock blocked the view of the driveway, but I saw it at the last second and made a sharp right onto a gently sloping hillside. I imagined that, in spring, the hillside was a field of wildflowers. That day, it was a carpet of frosty dew.

Once I reached the top of the incline, several structures came into view. Multiple steeples punctuated the roofline of the main building, but the customary place for a cross at the highest point over the chapel was occupied by a bronze rooster weathervane. The abbey seemed to say, "I'm Gothic. Don't be fooled by the rooster."

I parked in one of the few spots near the main doors. Mine was the only car, and I wondered if the place was still operational. It was eerily quiet. Could I be trespassing on private property? What was the worst thing that could happen? I might be attacked by a guard dog or shooed off the property by a crazed, arm-waving monk. I got out of the car and went up to the main door. When I pulled the handle, the door popped open with a neat little sucking sound.

A single candle lit the entryway, which meant I wasn't alone. While my eyes adjusted to the welcoming darkness, I listened to the creaking of the empty chapel. My footfalls echoed like bat wings, and I realized it was impossible to go undetected in that hyperactive acoustic. The stone floor and barren walls were to blame.

I sat halfway up the main aisle, relaxed my muscles, and exhaled. The pew groaned. The sound of my very presence shuffled in the air.

Incense inundated my nasal cavities. It was a pleasant sensation of an ancient aroma—frankincense and myrrh. The scent was heady and warm, and its juxtaposition to the sanctuary's cool atmosphere was compelling. My body flooded with wellbeing.

I jerked awake with the realization that I'd been sleeping. Objects stood out in relief against a backdrop of gloom. The visual experience reminded me of a Viewfinder I had as a kid. Dad had made a gold-clasped, red felt-lined wooden box that held the reels, tiny slides set into a wheel of cardboard that, when inserted into the Viewfinder, projected photos of scenes from around the world. There was Paris with an Eiffel Tower that jumped out in 3-D, the African Savanna, where elephants and tigers charged with bared teeth and bulging eyes, and the French wine country with row upon row of grapevines that dizzyingly exaggerated my depth perception.

Sitting in the chapel, I was gripped by a heightened sense of the 3-D-ness of the air that defined the space contained within the stone exterior. As if proving the existence of gravity, a slender candle in a red glass receptacle hung from the ceiling by three long, delicate chains. The flame glowed red, but it faded and bled out before touching anything tangible. The suspended redness was stunning, its halo of diffused light—significant.

An odd sensation crept along the back of my neck. Turning around, I saw a deep blue rosette stained glass window over the doors at the back of the chapel. The design was simple. Each petal was individually recessed into the thick stone wall. The solidness of the dark glass-in-stone flower struck an alluring balance with the suspended red flame.

As my awareness opened, I noticed things I hadn't seen at first. Up front and to one side sat a small alcove equipped with memorial candles, three of which were lit. A bare Quaker-type wooden table served as an altar. Other than the candles and a stained glass window of the Madonna with Child, the chapel lacked the usual religious paraphernalia: crucifixes, Bibles, hymnals. The minimalist décor resonated with me like sound waves vibrating through my bones.

My gaze settled on the red flame beacon. I breathed. A chamber in my heart stirred. I felt my lungs expand. A being was inside my chest and it had been there the whole time, waiting for me to notice. A sliver of the divine had ventured across an unseen barrier.

I realized that, like reflected moonlight on black water—proof of the sun's existence—beacons are signs that the soul really does exist.

Goldeness Tod

The weeks following my visit to the abbey, I dreamt about gold-clad, gold-skinned, living angels gliding about in the canopy of a deep-green pine forest; Christmas stockings overflowing with gold-foiled chocolate coins; and gold-saturated spiritual symbols: a Star of David, a pentagram, and a gold and blue-tinged Hamsa, a hand-shaped protective amulet.

From above, I saw myself sitting cross-legged, yogi-style, on my bed. A gold sphere hung midair above my head, and its crisp edge was separated by a sliver of daylight. The sphere was an upright plate made of hundreds of spinning petals flecked with gold. I woke from my dream filled with the most intense feeling of joy I'd ever known.

The following night, I had a dream without visuals. All I got was a voice—earthy and androgynous. *"Gedanken einer Goldeness Tod."* Imagine a Golden Death. It was my last dream before six dark months of insomnia.

Anne

"She's sitting by the woodstove in the music room . . . quietly reading through the Chopin Waltzes. We shouldn't disturb her."

For the first time since I'd known him, the melodious purr in Mr. Hanson's voice was lackluster. My heart felt as if it had stopped beating. After hanging up, I sat in my teaching chair and stared at the deep blue walls of my music studio.

I imagined Anne running her hands along the notes in the score—painstakingly, lovingly, longingly hearing melody and nuance better than if they'd resonated in actual air. It confirmed what she'd taught me forty years ago when I was an undergraduate at Hartt. She'd tapped her temple and said, "Carol dear, ninety-eight percent of playing a musical instrument takes place in the mind." Now, even though she no longer had the strength or coordination to sit at the piano, Chopin still inhabited her mind and her heart. I imagined her flipping the page to the next waltz. Feebly, she pushed her hands over the score in the trajectory of the phrases' shapes. Her fingers twitched in phantom motions over the notes. Her body swayed like a willow in a breeze, but her movements weren't necessarily in time with the music; rather, she evoked the piece by stirring it, rousing it into existence.

It was interesting that Anne chose the Waltzes with which to spend one of her final days on earth. It was tempting to question her choice. Certainly, there were more interesting pieces to revisit: the Ballades, Scherzos, Etudes, or Concertos. But even though Anne could easily "toss off" the most challenging repertoire by any composer, it was so *her* to seek refuge in the Waltzes. Melodic beauty is the beating heart of those pieces. Inner voices and sheer harmonic loveliness are the thermals on which the melodies soar. It was comforting to think of her in that sublime place.

Music for beauty's sake, for human betterment and global health, was something Anne loved to talk about. The wide scope of music's impact spread out from her persona in a soothing wave that washed over everyone in her sphere. She was hilarious, boisterous, playful, attentive, charismatic, and forthright. When cancer finally subdued the titanic sweep of her personality, her melodies remained intact in the hearts of all who knew her.

To me, Anne's clandestine meeting with Chopin that day intimated that she'd made a bold agreement with death: she'd give up her body if only she could retain her inner world until her last breath. Had she found peace at the end? I think she had. But even so, she confided in me that she'd hoped for "ten or twenty more years on the planet."

I spoke with her two days after they removed the tumor from her brain. Her southern enunciation of the diagnosis was like a haunting melody, "gli-o blast-o-ma, Carol. That's what I have in my brain. They assured me that removing the main tumor will give me more time." Her over-the-phone aura was simply, tragically—human. There was an uncharacteristic quality to her voice. An acceptance of nurturing that signified a reversal of roles. "Call anytime, Carol. *Please* do call."

The Yellow Warbler

"I wait."

The incantation created a faint breeze brushing past my lips. Maintaining a peripheral awareness of my surroundings, I homed in on the tree canopy. A cacophony of birdsong reverberated overhead, and I was lured into a dizzyingly seductive game of "find the source." It was a little like a horror movie as the treetops twirled around the glaring sun. I felt mocked. I shook my fist at the air.

It's easy to overlook the obvious. Anything can blend in if your mind doesn't accept what the eye sees. I scanned the trees and quickly found five species in a stand of saplings: a Western Tanager, Yellow-rumped Warbler, Downy Woodpecker, White-breasted Nuthatch, and a Black-capped Chickadee. It was an excellent find. But, my mind wasn't holding the image of a Great Horned Owl, and I walked right beneath one as it cooed like a puppy in its sleep. I was alert to sound though, and I recognized the little coo as owlish. Spinning around, I saw it sitting half asleep on a low limb of a gnarly oak.

Looking for birds foraging in the undergrowth gave my shoulders and neck a chance to relax. The minute I shifted my focus, there was a telltale shuffle in the leaves, and a Spotted Towhee brazenly darted across the trail and disappeared under a bush. It peeped, "I'm fast. I can cross the trail anytime I want." After that, all I saw of it was one red eye peeking out from under a bush. Gregarious Bewick's Wrens are found at eye level, and I easily spotted one attempting to corral a large brood of baby Bewick's, which noisily scampered around in the bramble. They bounced about as if they had springs for legs—*boing-boing-boing!* Like the towhee, the adult Bewick's flew ahead of me on the trail. It perched on a twig, raised its head, and flipped its tail feathers. I expected it to brandish a miniature rifle and say, "Who goes there?" I wasn't entirely wrong. The wren's song trumpeted from its wide-open beak as if it was proclaiming my day of reckoning. As a sign of respect, I averted my eyes while I passed. After one last triumphant outburst of tuneful song, the wren returned to its hopping, yipping, bumping young.

At the end of the trail, I came to an open field, which had an unobstructed view of the treetops. Birdsong resonated all around me. The highest leaves shook and shimmied like windup toys, and I kept in mind that bright birds can hide too. They're excellent yellow leaf, berry clump, or pool-of-light imitators. I simply had to convince one bird that it was safe to show itself—that I had no intention of eating it. I held my clasped hands to my chest. I waited. Then something started to happen. It looked like the sun was glinting off a leaf. But no. . . . A Yellow Warbler popped out from the leaves, perched on the tip of a branch, puffed out the straight-stitch orange lines on its tiny breast, and sang for me.

Part Five

Apt. 12C

Josef Raieff, my teacher at Juilliard, was a stocky, handsome, cigar-smoking romantic. He had the rare ability to sit down and play anything any of his students was working on: perfectly, fluidly, and with amazing beauty and ease—all without a glance at the music. Aside from the occasional wide-smiled compliment on my interpretive skills, he seldom discussed musical concepts with me. Instead, he helped develop a repertoire that challenged my interpretative mind, plus, he provided a plethora of invaluable fingerings that had been passed down through generations of teachers. At first glance, some of the bold fingerings seemed unnatural and fussy, but after fully committing to new advanced techniques, I experienced a freedom of facility that unexpectedly tamed the most daunting technical sections in my pieces. His masterful fingerings facilitated beauty of tone in Chopin, clarity in Mozart, bubbly articulation in Bach, and sheer speed whenever needed.

The summer months before beginning my graduate studies at Juilliard, we worked exclusively on Chopin Nocturnes. Two mornings a week, I played for Mr. Raieff while gazing out at the Hudson River from the window of his twelfth-floor apartment on West End Avenue.

Our focus was on tone production. At first, before discussing anything technical, he asked me to play right hand alone and to strive for a sustained, golden, singing tone. Each note was to artfully connect with its neighbors so as to create breathtakingly nuanced phrases. My teachers believed, as I did, that a pre-conceptualization of tone and phrasing is critical in creating a uniquely compelling sound. If a singing tone isn't evoked in the mind before depressing the key, it's left up to chance. The secrets of the nuanced physicality of tone production were imparted only after calling upon my natural facility.

When he demonstrated at the keyboard, Mr. Raieff's eloquence circumvented words. His velvety tone glimmered in his eyes, alighted in his hands, and was conjured through the pads of his fingers. He encouraged me to observe his touch up close and then to experiment with my version of it. I was not to imitate, but to find my own sound, one suited to my unique hands, imagination, and temperament.

"Where's your tone, Carol?" Mr. Raieff's raspy voice penetrated my concentrated state. "Use your pads. Activate your first joints!"

Fourth finger on E-flat, slow subtle contact with the keybed, arm weight gentle but firm, pad caressing the key, first joint gently activating, then the arm lifting while the fingertip maintains relaxed contact with the keybed. There it was—sustained, singing tone!

"Excellent, dearheart. Now you're ready for two notes in a row." The glimmering eyes, the mischievous smile, the cigar stub clenched between his teeth. "Now your brilliant technique and musical heart have a worthy companion." Mr. Raieff reached for a whiskey.

As my first days at Juilliard approached, the summer of Chopin Nocturnes came to a gentle close. The last hour was spent on slow releases, which seamlessly flow from the motions that produce a sustained, singing tone: the rising arm, the yielding wrist, the fingertip maintaining constant unforced contact with the surface of the key as it rises from the keybed, the gradual controlled ascent of the key itself as it slowly approaches its place in line with its neighbors, and finally, the inaudible moment of letting go.

My hand was a Bittern stealthily lifting its pea-soup-green leg as it moves undetected farther into the reeds.

Stepping out onto West End Avenue, I glanced up at the façade of the building that housed apartment 12C, where I learned that, not only does an unhindered technique best serve the music, it's also a guardian of beauty. Whether performed in mountain-range-shaped half notes or gamboling strings of sixteenths, golden tone is achieved by the unification of heart, mind, and body.

Like the late-morning mist rising from the Hudson, the enigma that surrounded tone production was slowly demystifying.

Carol Rich

Mystical Fingerings

In the book, *The Art of Quartet Playing: The Guarneri Quartet in conversation with David Blum,* cellist David Soyer tells a story about the quartet hiring a clairvoyant to contact Beethoven. The idea was to discern the meaning of an unusual notation Beethoven used in his String Quartet, *Grosse Fuge,* Op. 133. The notation is a series of two-note slurs, all on the same pitch, with a staccato mark on the second note. In order to facilitate the meeting, Soyer provided the clairvoyant with a hand-written copy of the notation, followed by a big question mark.

When the clairvoyant returned to report on her findings, she said that Beethoven was easy to contact, but he was ill-tempered and frustrated that she didn't speak German. Even so, when she showed him Soyer's note, Beethoven nodded and let out a series of interpretive groans, "*Uhh*-uhh . . . *uhh*-uhh."

This topic was of particular interest to me because the same notation is found in Beethoven's Piano Sonata, Op. 110. Mr. Raieff advised me to play the gesture like a series of groans (his words exactly), and showed me a special technique and fingering to create the unique effect on the piano. It involved striking the second note in each two-note slur while the key was still ascending. It took practice.

Uhh-uhh . . . *uhh*-uhh. *Knock, knock, knock, knock.*

Among Giants

In 1979, my first year as a Master's candidate, Leonard Bernstein guest conducted the Juilliard Orchestra in Mahler's Third Symphony. As a kid, I was a faithful viewer of the televised Young People's Concerts hosted by Bernstein from 1958-72. I'd also seen him conduct the New York Philharmonic live many times. Now I was watching him from six feet away.

The rehearsal room was packed with student observers, including the ones who rarely left the practice room or ventured out from the stacks in the library. I wedged myself among a throng of kindred pianists directly behind the strikingly beautiful, emotive, charismatic "Lenny." Being in his energy field was like taking a train ride that zipped through the landscape while an unseen force tethered our conductor to a track of unwavering musical intention. Wringing every drop of meaning from the notes on the page, he fell to one knee and double-fisted his baton heavenward as sweat poured over his impassioned face. Coming from a less sincere conductor, his gesticulations would've seemed overblown. But this was the real thing. His emotional display came across as strength. Lenny was generous. He never, not even once, scowled or frowned at the musicians. Every moment was devotion to the music.

From 1979-83, I had the honor of being one of the staff accompanists at Juilliard. I played in the studios of Julius Baker, retired principal flutist of the New York Philharmonic; William Lincer, retired principal violist, also of the New York Phil; and on the rare occasion, in the studio of premier violin teacher Dorothy Delay. Lincer's studio was next door to Delay's, so I witnessed how her students waited, sometimes all day, for their violin lessons. The lengthy wait was legendary, but so was she.

One morning, I arrived at Lincer's studio to play for a full day of viola lessons. On my way in, I nodded hello to eleven-year-old prodigy star Midori, who was warming up for her lesson with Delay. It was the year of Midori's New York Philharmonic debut, and when I emerged for my one o'clock lunch break, I was surprised to find her still waiting—practicing perfectly in-tune double-stop parallel sixths up and down the fingerboard. She was still there when I came back from lunch. Years later, I accompanied her in preparation for a concerto appearance and asked what it was like to wait so long for her lessons. She said, "The longer the wait, the better prepared."

With fully sprouted eyebrows, dense mustache, and black-framed glasses, violist William Lincer looked like a wide-bodied Groucho Marx. His students and studio accompanists adored his good-humored, easy-going nature. Lincer was our omniscient dad. A well-established depression in the red sofa cushion revealed where he'd spent half a century honing the skills of the world's finest violists. Lessons were open for all of his students to observe, and sometimes there'd be three or four violists listening in with pencils and scores ready to receive his wisdom. The viola repertoire isn't what one would call vast, so the same Brahms Sonatas, Schubert Arpeggione Sonata, Walton or Bartók Concerto would be studied by several of his students simultaneously. Unlike pianists, who claim ownership over the repertoire they're currently studying—even to the point of breaking off friendships if someone dare violate the unspoken code of exclusivity—violists don't have that option. As their pianist-collaborator, I found that the repetition cut down on practice time, providing the opportunity for me to explore unique voicing, phrasing, and character suited to each player's personality.

Violists are soulful and good-natured. Flute players are bouncy and fast-paced. Every day in Julius Baker's studio revealed a succession of exuberant flutists whose talents eclipsed the student before them. They all had flawless technique, unearthly speed, angelic phrasing, scintillating tone, and Herculean endurance. If they didn't come to Juilliard with it, Julie taught them strength of tone. I had no idea flutes could produce such solid sound.

Julie had a disconcerting habit of squeezing onto the piano bench with me during lessons. Fortunately, the hearing in my right ear wasn't affected by the sustained high notes he loved to play just inches from my head. Opera singers did this same awful thing when I played for their masterclasses. They'd put their hand on my shoulder and sing—full voice—those ear-splitting, air-crackling sounds meant for huge halls.

Julius Baker was known for his scintillating silver tone, which sprang forth from the middle of the orchestra and soared out to the audience. I admired his sound many times as a young concert-goer. Playing in his studio, I learned that, up close, his tone was breathtakingly beautiful, but also a bit fuzzy. It was an illusion unique to Julie's style of playing, one that became the tone of an angel when heard from the audience.

One day, Julie and I were thigh to uncomfortable thigh on the piano bench in his studio, when he lifted his flute to his lips and blasted out the highest, most screechy note I'd ever heard. His face turned red with exertion. He burst out laughing. "It's a high D, Carol. I discovered a new note! Listen . . ." (Just in case I missed it the first time.) Now, decades later, D, plus a few higher notes, is part of the regular flute range. Even though it temporarily short-circuited my brain, Julie's discovery was groundbreaking.

𝄋

One afternoon, I was in the Juilliard elevator when the doors slid open and in stepped Mikhail Baryshnikov. He wore sweatpants and a tight fitting, muscle-revealing, black sleeveless top. His skin glimmered with sweat. He leaned against the elevator wall, smiled, and said, "Hello." It sounded more like "Chello," as if he was clearing his throat. I managed to squeak out, "Hello," even though I was on the verge of a major coronary event. There is such a thing as charisma.

𝄋

My father kept a small, black, gold-edged autograph book. It's a microcosmic representation of time spent among musical giants, most of which either he or Birdie had met during their Juilliard years. Some of the highlights: Pianist Josef Hofmann, 1931 with handwritten musical snippet. Violinist Jascha Heifetz, 1931. Horowitz, 1931. Juilliard president Ernest Hutcheson, 1931. Theodore Steinway, 1931, with hand-drawn Steinway insignia. Editor and Liszt's student Alexander Siloti, 1931. (My students love knowing that, since my teacher, Josef Raieff, studied with Siloti, it makes them fourth-generation Lisztians.) Conductor Fritz Reiner, 1931. Pianist Dame Myra Hess, 1932. Composer/pianist Leopold Godowsky, 1932, with handwritten music. Caricaturist Hirschfeld, with original self-portrait, the semblance of which could've been my father. Cellist Gregor Piatigorsky, 1933. Pianist Artur Schnabel, 1933.

Carefully turning the well-preserved pages of the autograph book, my fingertips find the indents left in the paper where enthusiastic conductors and pianists underscored their names. I admire the unique placement of their contributions on the page: some neatly positioned in a corner, while others, nearly illegibly signed, fill entire pages with diagrams, musical notations, and even personal anecdotes.

I'm struck with awe by the full-blooded musical heritage of my father's generation. Imagining my youthful father or grandmother approaching the greatest of all time to ask for their autograph gives me a thrill. But my smile is tinged with regret. I so wish I'd followed through when I was at Juilliard.

∽

In1980, I performed in a shared recital at Alice Tully Hall at Lincoln Center, which sat across the plaza from Juilliard. The recital was part of the weekly Students at Juilliard Presents series. My program consisted of six Preludes from Op. 11 by Scriabin, Liszt's *Frühlingsnacht* and 10th Hungarian Rhapsody, two Fairy Tales by Medtner, and *Étincelles* by Moszkowski. Ten years after Birdie recommended that I look into Medtner, the Fairy Tales were finally on my program. I'm sure my face reflected astonishment when Mr. Raieff suggested I learn them. He said, "They're gems, Carol. And the E-flat makes a dazzler of an encore." I'd inherited Birdie's Medtner scores, but I'd never even read through them. She and Mr. Raieff were right. They were perfect for me. The program was made up of short-form pieces—miniatures—impactful, charming dazzlers. The Liszt Hungarian Rhapsody was the only piece of any length, and served as the program's anchor. The repertoire, including the Medtner, was Horowitzian.

Alice Tully Hall was cavernous, and aside from playing *Rhapsody in Blue* in the Vienna Opera House when I was seventeen, it was my first real foray into playing solo repertoire in a hall of its size and significance. I had some nerves during my ten-minute warm-up on stage that morning, but once I'd made my long entrance walk to the piano during the actual performance, I just wanted to play. There was nowhere I'd rather have been.

The interplay between performer and audience is unique in a vast space such as Alice Tully Hall, and I quickly learned the power of evoking soft, sustained tone. I felt the listener lean in. My hands and mind were steady. I found control. My shared recital that day set me up for all future solo and concerto performances. Sincere musical communication between audience and player is addictive.

I knew that Mr. Raieff considered the performance a test of nerves, concentration, and musical commitment. Afterwards, his eyes twinkled when he asked me to lunch at O'Neal's Balloon, just across Broadway. We had "the talk," which, to Juilliard Masters students, meant discussing the future. Will there be an agent? Where will my specific talents be best used? Where is my heart taking me? These were easy questions, and my answers were the same as they were two years ago when I first started at Juilliard. Like the armloads of recordings I took home as a kid, I wanted it all. Yet, it was important that solo repertoire retain its place at the center of my studies, where it would perpetually rekindle my sense of personal style and refine my technique. I'd continue teaching, studying, and pouring myself into whatever genre of classical music wound up on my piano rack. As gratifying as my Alice Tully Hall solo performance was, my resolve hadn't softened. No need for an agent.

It was finals week. After finishing a grueling piano literature exam, I had one precious hour before my last lesson with Mr. Raieff. I was ravenous, but apparently I wasn't the only one in need of extra fuel for year-end activities. The student cafeteria was slammed. My stomach was growling *forte, con fuoco* by the time I reached the front of the line. Then, world-renowned pianist Earl Wilde nudged his way in front of me. He'd detoured past the clearly posted menu and ordering counter and opted instead for a long discussion with the server.

The delay cost me valuable pre-lesson warm-up time, but more importantly, it cost me my perfectly charred grilled cheese sandwich that I watched dangle from the chef's tongs before it was unceremoniously plopped into the trash. My stomach churned. While waiting for a second perfectly charred grilled cheese sandwich, I stared out the oversize windows and watched a sailboat glide down Broadway. It turned out to be the original African Queen, manned by actors portraying Katharine Hepburn and Humphrey Bogart.

The grilled cheese was black, gooey, and fuel-packed. My farewell lesson was stellar.

❧

The day of my final graduate requirement at Juilliard had finally arrived—the piano jury. I'd prepared three hours of music from which the panel would select forty-five minutes for me to play. Ten minutes before stepping onstage, I was told which sections of which pieces I'd be performing, and in what order. My jury repertoire consisted of the Bach English Suite in G Minor, all seven movements, with improvised embellishments, including the devilish Gigue, which I performed all *staccato* with both repeats; sections of Schubert's Posthumous Sonata in A Major; three Medtner Fairy Tales; Scriabin's Piano Sonata No. 9; and as much of Liszt's Hungarian Rhapsody No. 10 as time would allow. The last-minute notification of selected repertoire stood up to its notoriously nerve-racking reputation, but by pushing my concentration to the max, I discovered a deep well of focus and power.

The jury took place in Paul Hall, Juilliard's recital hall, and was presented to the entire piano faculty, who sat in the shadows of the last rows. The only indication that time was up would be the tap of a pencil from one of the jurors. There'd be no conversation between pieces, and without an actual audience, there'd be no applause. Still, I was aware of Mr. Raieff's strong, supportive persona amongst the panel of his brilliant Juilliard professor peers. I briefly thought of Rosina Lhévinne. Then I focused on Bach.

Forty-five minutes went by quickly, and the glissando section of the 10th Hungarian Rhapsody was excruciatingly close. If the signal happened before that, I'd have to fight my instincts to keep playing. I prepared my reflexes to lift my hands from the keyboard mid-phrase.

I also activated my tiny-noise receptors in order to hear a pencil tap over the intricately complex rhythmic episode I was playing.

I heard a faint *tap-tap-tap* in unison with Mr. Raieff's raspy voice. "Let her finish. You've got to hear the glisses. Keep playing, Carol!"

As a gift to my beloved teacher, I gave his delicately fancy glissando tricks extra finesse. When I came to the powerful double glissando section, a recent memory gave me a final burst of strength.

I was in my initial rendering of the first eight measures of the Rhapsody's knuckle-busting coda when one of Juilliard's resident wise guys in the adjacent practice room tore through it at full volume and speed. It was then that I realized there would always be pianists both better and worse than me. At the time, the thought was both humbling and slightly humiliating. But ultimately, realizing my place in the world of pianists was comforting. I had something unique to offer. After the wise guy was done spewing "my" piece, he followed it up with a door slam, and then he rapped out of a perfunctory "ha-ha" on my practice room door. I resumed my study, not realizing at the time that Liszt's #10 would top off my final Masters jury, and that it would become one of my signature pieces. The heavy-fisted wise guy would've benefited greatly from Mr. Raieff's refined glissando techniques.

Lifting my hands from the final chord, I turned to the darkened hall and said, "Thank you." My student days at Juilliard were over.

My time at Juilliard was accompanied by a suspicion that, even though I was valued by my teachers, they were on to me. There were days when I wondered if my being there was all a terrific mistake. Juilliard is known for advancing the solo careers of musicians of the highest caliber, and even though my ever-growing, technique-expanding repertoire was on par with the charismatic students destined for big solo careers, my nature was shy and reclusive. My life's trajectory would never take me on a journey parallel to theirs. Plus, I lacked the prerequisite thirst for the spotlight and self-promotion. Still, all of my previous teachers agreed with Mr. Raieff when he called me a natural musician and an inventive interpreter. He encouraged me to follow my instincts about my career choices, whether solo or collaborative.

The fact that I'd been given my teacher's blessing to pursue my eclectic musical interests helped me realize that all of my mentors at Juilliard acknowledged and supported me *because* I was suited for a richly diverse musical career in conjunction with solo concertizing. My musical destiny opened up like a river delta reaching across fields of symphonic, ballet, chamber music, vocal and instrumental collaboration, and choral work. I was free to honor and nurture my love of practice and study. Surrounding myself with knowledge-thirsty students, I refined my skills as a teacher. I learned that, going out into the world as a multi-faceted ambassador of Juilliard, I could represent my school with genuine pride.

In 1981, I crossed the stage in Alice Tully Hall, this time, to accept my Master of Music degree from Aaron Copland. His handshake, like his music and his smile, was firm yet tender. The slight pressure of his fingers against my palm left a lasting impression, one that infused my approach to music, as well as my philosophy of teaching, with reverence and patience.

Carol Rich

First Ride

Dad's red face bounded along beside me. "Ready? I'm gonna let go now."

The green streamers on the handlebars fluttered beneath my forearms. I kept my feet moving.

It felt like Dad wasn't pushing me along anymore, and when I glanced to my left, my pulse surged. I was on my own. As I pedaled, my mind's eye saw him behind me, hands hanging to his sides, palms out, as if wishing me forward with the strength of his heart.

I wobbled past a small indent in the pavement and cruised down the dead-end street. It was a straight shot to the edge of the woods where, last autumn, Bob had fallen into a nasty patch of giant skunk cabbage growing in a stream just beyond a stand of saplings. I pedaled past three wood and glass houses, the newest additions to our split-level neighborhood. My eyes had taken a while to adjust to their modern design, but I grew to appreciate how comfortably the houses nestled into the woods.

Squirrels skittered noisily around a tree. Their nails clicked and scraped the rough bark as they scurried up the trunk and then sprang, trampoline-like, from lithe branch to lithe branch. Bevies of red and gold leaves fluttered free from massive elms and oaks, whose limbs opened and spread like thick brown umbrella skeletons overhead. Then, from way back behind me, I heard Dad shout, "Hit the brakes! Skunk cabbage!"

Pushing back on the pedals, I stepped off. Dad flung his arms into the air. He looked like a large bird taking flight—liberating itself from the earth's gravity in two majestic flaps.

I turned the bike around, and under my own power this time, made the handlebar streamers lift into the wind.

Carol Rich

Backstage

No other performance venue could compare with the ambience, intimacy, and mystique of Carnegie Recital Hall. Discovering the Steinway's secret tone, craving the adrenalin which surged through me in waves—these were the glance, sigh, and abandon of a life-changing affair.

My musical collaborator, a cellist by the name of Loretta O'Sullivan, had left immediately after rehearsal, and I was alone with the hall. My usual post-rehearsal euphoria was magnified by simply sitting at the piano in such an esteemed space. My skin tingled. I yearned. I played to the empty seats. Bach.

Afterwards, finally opening the mystery door in my dressing room, I peered down a dimly lit hallway that appeared to reach the entire length of a city block. Putting a wedge between the door and sash, I left the off-white, gold-trimmed décor of Carnegie Recital Hall and entered a surprisingly narrow, shell-white corridor. It was like being in the hollow bone of a bird.

There were several lookalike doors along the opposite wall, but none had signage, and all were locked—except for one. Turning the doorknob, I entered a red-carpeted, wide-ramped passageway. Suddenly, I knew exactly where I was. I crossed the deserted corridor, pulled aside a deep purple curtain, and stepped into one of the priciest seating areas in Carnegie Hall: the first-tier box seats nearest the stage. A single light—the ghost light—cast an elongated globe of white luminescence on center stage.

I reminisced about how several years earlier, Melvin and I had taken a short road trip from West Hartford to the city to attend a recital series of Itzhak Perlman and Vladimir Ashkenazy playing the ten Beethoven Violin Sonatas at Carnegie Hall. We sat in the box seats directly above where I was standing, which gave me an unobstructed, aerial view of Ashkenazy's hands, as well as the interplay between the two men. When I mentioned to Melvin how easy it would be to throw flowers onto the stage from our perch, he left and returned minutes later with a bouquet of daffodils. I didn't ask where he managed to find the flowers during the recital, but I assumed it was the same magic kingdom from which he was able to dig up two adjacent parking spots long enough for the hearse. During the bows at the end of the recital, I javelined the daffodils onto the stage, where they joined dozens of bouquets that gathered at Perlman's and Ashkenazy's feet.

The box seat in the tier above my head was also the location where I attended Ashkenazy's solo recital on April 1, 1977, which included works of Scriabin on one half and Rachmaninoff on the other. That night, I went alone—equipped with a single rose to toss into the barrage of flowers, the outpouring of love, that rained down onto the stage afterwards. The power of Ashkenazy's musical presence in that performance still resonates within my bones.

Loretta's and my performance on Carnegie Recital Hall's smaller stage didn't elicit flowers at our feet, but receiving multiple curtain calls allowed us to play two encores. Afterwards, I had one more thing to do before heading to the after-party at the Russian Tea Room next door on 57th Street. But before that, I had to wait for the congratulatory throngs in the Recital Hall to disperse.

Then I was alone again, and I threw my arms into the sweet air of success. I tossed my bag over my shoulder, pushed open the dressing room door, and revisited the narrow hallway, where I crossed the plush red carpet by the box seats. The acoustics in the passageway were more muffled and slightly stuffier than after rehearsal that morning. I cautiously pulled back the purple curtain.

Immediately, a small huddle of men blocked my way. They were three versions of intimidation: slicked-back hair, black suits, skinny ties over dark colored shirts. I actually had to stifle the words, "Are you guys goons?" They reeked of cigarette smoke and strong cologne. When one of them asked me what I wanted, "You need some-m, lady?" I told him I was just looking around. He grunted and signaled to his friends to relax.

Then I heard his velvety voice. On stage, where the ghost light had been, Frank Sinatra was sitting on a tall stool in a pool of cool blue/white light. He was delivering one of his iconic ballads. Smoke rose from a cigarette dangling from his hand, and a hat tilted to one side cast a shadow over his face. The band was phenomenal, almost as engrossing as Sinatra himself . . . almost. Everything about the performance was the class act you'd imagine it to be. Even the audience was classy: an older set of women and men dressed to the "nines" with women in furs and men sporting silk scarves. The head "goon" shifted in his shiny black, silver-tipped shoes. After one more song, I let myself out.

It was common in those days for music students to sneak into the big halls. It was like being a member of a clan of like-minded people. It was a peek into the future—a sampling of possibility. The next time I was at Carnegie Recital Hall, then, as an audience member, I snuck into the big hall one last time. Pulling back the purple curtain, I saw the Pointer Sisters singing *Boogie Woogie Bugle Boy.* A lot more happens at Carnegie Hall than classical music.

Twirt

"Places!"

Several dancers scattered into the wings. The onstage lights dimmed to an exquisite shade of glacier-ice blue. Lifting my hands over the opening notes, I conceptualized my first sound.

Then came the faraway *click—click—click* of the stage manager's cue. After waiting a beat, I unleashed a rumbling, angry D Minor chord. I was being mic'd, making the tremolo enormous and terrifying. I imagined hundreds of audience members jumping in their seats. I'd gotten their attention.

To my right, the violinist lifted her bow and leaned into an impassioned melody. Someone was going to die tonight, and it wasn't going to be pretty.

A full minute passed while we navigated the music's emotionally devastated landscape. Then, as I turned my head for a cue from the violinist, the curtain went up. A telltale odor from the audience wafted over the footlights: perfume, cigarette residue, smelly feet—like skunk cabbage.

My chest filled with knowing. I sensed a shift in the audience's attention away from the violinist and me to the dancers sitting stage left. The ballerina's toe slid along the floorboards just as the music became seductively playful. She was a bad girl—you could tell from the angle of her foot. My eyes were fixed on the score, but my peripheral awareness was fully activated. The dancer's toe governed the tempo. She had long lines, long legs, and clean articulation—a musician's dream dancer. Her male partner was lyrical, beautiful, and responsive to her every whim.

Their love was doomed. We all knew it. Yet, the violin sang so sweetly, so purely, we were almost lured into believing that the story would end differently this time.

The dancer's leg lifted her skirts into the air as she twirled around her partner. I always notated choreography in my score, and I'd accidently written "twirt" in that spot, making me smile every time I played it. I wondered if anyone in the audience noticed my grin.

The dancers moved with fluid freedom, and I was the rudder keeping us from spinning out of control. Fullness of movement, not speed, was the goal. We were perfectly in sync. Taken in by the beauty of the moment, I let my gaze drift from the score to follow the dancers' line. It was okay. I knew the progression of chords well—it was my favorite part of the dance.

The dancers were fully impassioned. She slid to the floor and slinked snakelike downstage of the possessed violinist. The male dancer grimaced as he finally succumbed to his seductress, fully collapsing into her ill-fated embrace. They writhed and twisted downstage until stopping mere inches from the edge.

Focusing on accuracy and dramatic timing, I released the final chord and my arms rose into the air. The stage went to black.

The curtain's rapid descent sounded like an elephant on a zip-line. Yet, in the ensuing moment of utter darkness, the quiet power of the dance continued to surge through me. I raced into the wings.

I'm short of breath. My throat constricts. Things of the world—material objects—are forgotten. Waves of sadness and longing flood over me, but I'm not sure why. It has something to do with loss. If I had a blanket, I'd draw it up to my chin.

My chest heaves with emotion. My eyes sting. I yearn for a view of the forest or the ocean. The longing manifests in a single sob.

My eyes close and my father is there. He's conveying a message: don't be afraid, don't fight it, it is possible to make the journey through darkness with grace.

I listen to the hissing silence in my head. I'm afraid that if I open my eyes, I'll forget what he said. I'm afraid that I'll find out he was never there.

The muted roar of applause from behind the thick curtain jolted me back to the present. I remembered that a second after the curtain had thudded to the deck, I'd gotten the heck out of the way. My sense of sight and hearing played back their memory of what happened next: the onstage lights turned tutu pink and the crew swarmed onto the stage. Audio cables were detached and the piano was slid behind the upstage curtain leg, ready for tomorrow night's performance. The dancers hurried offstage to their pre-bow spots. I grabbed my music and glasses, and wiped my eyes.

Now, upstage, behind the main curtain, the crew was busy setting the stage for the next dance. But in front of the curtain, toward the house, white-hot spotlights illuminated the dancers as they bowed to the cheering audience. My chest heaved with post-performance euphoria while I waited in my favorite spot, just steps out of view, in the wings. Then, sweat glistening on her arms, chest, and face, the prima ballerina fluttered over to the violinist and me, and escorted us to center stage.

Bowing toward the roaring crowd, I recalled the brief moment of exquisite darkness when my father came to me.

Carol Rich

A Preface to Love Letters

I never told my father what he meant to me—how I'm not as lonely or sad as I would've been without the image of his hands, the silent stability of his love, or the sustaining underpinning of our shared musical life.

As a child, it was my nature to be closed off, shy, and happily hidden inside my observer's persona. It was my father's nature too. We contented ourselves with rich, separate-but-linked, inward-directed existences that were moored to music and to one another.

Every night, after putting away our four-hand music, he'd retreat to the den to listen to WQXR, one of the four classical music stations we had in New York. When I finished my practicing and homework, I'd look in on him to find him asleep in his leather swivel chair. His head was flopped to one side and his hand still held a pen pointing to the swooping line it'd made across the *Times* crossword. His reading glasses were poised to fall off the tip of his nose. His bushy eyebrows took the shape of question marks.

I couldn't recall ever having had a meaningful, non-music-related conversation with my father, and for a long time, I craved words—the kind that would reveal how we *felt*.

Even though Dad had performance degrees in organ from Juilliard, he relinquished his musical career in order to fulfill, what he believed to be, his family duty—as his mother had done for him and his sister. He got a business degree from City College of New York, and then got a "job job" working downtown in the garment district at a clothing company called Stretchini, a subsidiary of Bobby Brooks. It saddened me when I realized what he'd given up for us kids.

One time, when I was about ten years old, Dad took me to work with him. We rode the Hudson Line from Dobbs Ferry to Grand Central, where I got to put my subway token in the slot before boarding a train to the Garment District on 36th Street. After we climbed up the subway stairs, Dad grabbed my hand and we dashed between throngs of workmen in sweaty tee shirts, suspenders, and dress pants as they pushed overloaded clothing racks down the streets and sidewalks. While Dad went to meetings, I sat in his fancy swivel chair and played with the adding machine. The long, calculation-peppered ribbons of paper made a perfect souvenir of my day with Dad.

୨

My studio apartment in The Bretton, on West 86th and Broadway, took six months to find, and even though it was small, it was all mine. The building was inhabited by artist types, mostly musicians. I could practice as late and for as long as I wanted. One of my adjoining neighbors was a classical bassist, and the other was a music producer who worked out of his apartment. Earphones were permanently attached to his head, and I never heard a sound from him the entire four years that I lived there. I would've thought his place was empty except that his door was perpetually propped open.

Mine was one of only four apartments in the hotel-turned-apartment building that had a shallow balcony accessed by two ill-fitting oversize windows. If I leaned way out over the wrought iron railing and looked downtown, I could see the Empire State Building. My balcony was my backyard, where I tended pots of red geraniums in spring and built snow-people on those rare, wonderful, wintery days when the entire city, including the subways, would shut down on account of the weather. The apartment had 9-foot ceilings and was affordable too. Being a rent-controlled building, the rent could go up only 3% between tenants, and since my predecessor was there for fourteen years, I paid a modest $450 a month. That was in the early '80s. At street level, on Broadway itself, there was a broiled-barbequed-roasted chicken place that sent saliva-inducing aromas wafting into my apartment all the way up on the tenth floor. It was chicken, all day, every day. I was perpetually hungry.

In true hotel style, the Bretton had apartment-designated slots behind a counter in the lobby, and mail was hand-delivered by the building manager. I had two phone lines: one was the traditional type and the other was an in-house line. I could pick up the handset of the bulky, black phone and ask the front desk to connect me with, say, my friend Wolf in 1206. One day, the in-house phone rang and a guy with a heavy British accent said, "Please get off the blower! I'm trying to talk to my sister in England!"

I lived at Broadway and West 86th for four charmed years.

When I was four, we moved from Flushing, Queens to Ardsley, a small town in Westchester County, twenty miles north of the city. As I grew up, our class trips took us to places like The Guggenheim, MoMA (The Museum of Modern Art), the Metropolitan Museum of Art, The Cloisters, The Blue Note in the Village, and Broadway theaters where I saw the original casts in *Hair*, *A Chorus Line*, *1776*, *You're a Good Man Charlie Brown*, and *Hello Dolly*, which had two versions—one with Carol Channing and one with Pearl Bailey, who ate an entire chicken onstage during her opening monologue.

My family spent Christmas Eves attending the midnight service at St. Thomas Episcopal Church on 5th Avenue. As a child, I was struck by the purity of the vibrato-less, idyllic intonation of The St. Thomas Choir for Men and Boys, the splashy organ playing, and the heady incense delivered from a swinging pendulum held by a white-and-gold clad priest.

I had private music theory and composition lessons provided free by the public school. Ardsley High was small. There were only ninety kids in my graduating class, but we had two choirs, an orchestra, an award-winning concert band, and a music theory teacher. As a result, I entered my undergraduate music courses at Hartt at the third-year, junior level.

It followed that I could've gotten my Master's from Juilliard in one year, but I'd waited so long to get there, I wanted to extend the experience. I took as many upper-level classes as my inheritance from Birdie could afford. After graduation, I retained my Staff Accompanist designation for two more years, which, even though I could've received higher fees privately, provided job security and much appreciated continuity. The stacks of music on my piano grew to new heights. On the rare free afternoon, I met up with friends on the steps of MoMA, took the subway to the Blue Note in the Village, trekked over the Brooklyn Bridge, and took the Hudson Line to the Cloisters. I was a regular at Zabar's, H&H Bagels, and Empire Szechuan—all right there on the twenty-block walk down Broadway between my apartment and Juilliard, at Lincoln Center.

One day in my mid-twenties, I realized I didn't have enough cash to fill a bag of groceries. It was as if a deep and lovely enchantment had come to a sudden end.

❧

My stomach rumbled. Holding a quarter between thumb and ring finger, I scanned up and down Broadway for a place to buy the perfect bite. It would be like fitting a gourmet meal on a teaspoon. A rush of sizzling pain shot through the thick membrane inside my skull, and I steadied myself against the newsstand where I'd just bought Tuesday's *New York Times,* the science edition. Suddenly, a full orchestra was playing Tchaikovsky's Piano Concerto in my head. Grimacing, I envisioned the limbic core in my brain as it released the lava flow of music.

"You okay, Charlie girl?" The furrows in the news guy's forehead were deeper than usual. He placed his hand on a stack of *Rolling Stones*. His weathered skin was like a rhino's, but his fingernails were smooth and shiny like alabaster.

"I'm fine. Thanks, Paz. See you tomorrow."

Our conversation was done in time to hear the piano launch into its majestic chords, which bounded along the keyboard in giant leaps.

Rubbing the quarter between my fingers, I crossed 67th Street and hopped up onto the sidewalk. But, the toe of my black zip-up boots caught the lip of the curb and my bag and I were flung across the pavement. Schubert Sonatas, Liszt Etudes, the *Times,* pencils, eyeglass case, wallet, and keys fanned out amongst a forest of legs. The velocity of the fall forced tears from my eyes. Scrambling to gather the contents of the bag, I pushed away several people who offered help.

"Thanks, I've got it," I mumbled.

I imagined that the tingling sensation in my head meant that a tear-blurred memory was being implanted in my mind. The memory would look like this: The Schubert, the cover of which was permanently torn from the body of the score, was spattered with grime; a stranger's lip gloss, most likely on the sidewalk before the fall, was now a stowaway among newly sharpened pencils; my wallet was sitting freakishly on its side, right there on the New York City sidewalk.

The music scores went into the bag first—irreplaceable fingerings and notations from multiple teachers were to be cherished. Then in went the piano glasses and wallet. I held a tissue to the growing blood stain on the shin of my pants.

"Is this yours? Are you okay?" The slender fingers that held out the quarter were like petals on a wilting lily.

"Thanks. Embarrassed. But I'll be fine." By the time I looked up, the back of the stranger's tan raincoat had been absorbed into the crowd of downtown-bound pedestrians.

I exchanged my twenty-five cents for a two-inch square of dark-chocolate-covered marshmallow from Zabar's candy counter. Four bites of bliss.

ℐ

Up to that point, my professional life had been predetermined by my collaborators' managers. But in order to pay the bills, retaining my staff accompanist position post-graduation meant having to play for a larger roster of soloists. After two more years in financial limbo and a life-clarifying, near-death experience on tour—our plane's engine cut out on takeoff, sending us swooping down low over the roofs in downtown Memphis before swooping up again and eventually making a quick U-turn—I reluctantly relinquished my staff accompanist position and took on a longer roster of professional soloists. My income skyrocketed almost immediately, but all of my time was consumed by practicing, rehearsing, and performing. Riding the jostling subway to and from concerts became treasured time for reflection. Despite my newfound security, it felt more than ever that I was on a fast and furious track to nowhere. I was a whirligig—appearing to be going places, but actually remaining stationary. I was booked out two years in advance. Yet, my post-Juilliard success as a collaborative pianist hadn't brought me the satisfaction I wanted and expected from my music. When I wasn't playing, my heart was as cavernous as a subway tunnel. I needed *more,* but I hadn't a clue what that would look like or what to do about it. Something had to give. I seriously contemplated leaving the city.

Love Letters

Then Dad's letters started coming. About one a week. I was dumbfounded by the outpouring of repentance and adoration that spilled off the pages I held in my trembling hands. I'm sure that for him, his purge was cathartic. Of course, he'd want a response. He deserved one. It broke my heart that I couldn't give it to him. I knew how to pour my soul into music, but my solitary focus had left me crippled when it came to verbalizing vulnerabilities like loneliness, need, and love.

The letters kept coming. He didn't wait for a reply. I read them, but only when I felt ready to take in the intensity of his words. Some letters sat unopened for days. When I did read them, I was faced with page after page of bitter regret. He'd placed each treasured word on yellow, narrow-lined paper.

My precious daughter—dear, sweet, talented Carol,

I love you. My love for you fills my heart to overflowing, and I'm unable to contain it another day. Forgive me if the burden of my words is too much. I hope it makes us both stronger.

Dad

A memory wormed its way out of my heart. The family was on an outing, walking around a small local lake. The fog was so thick it completely shrouded Mom and the boys walking up ahead. All of a sudden, I felt Dad take my hand in his, and a flurry of intensity passed between us, one that was too profound for the seven-year-old me to absorb. I wasn't used to being held or touched in that way. I clearly remember waiting a few minutes to see if I could grow to like it, but I didn't.

Standing in my apartment in New York, yet another letter written on a sheet of yellow paper shook in my hands. Shame flooded my entire being. Even as a kid, I should've tried harder to let him in. But I reminded myself that at the time, the unexpected touch of his hand roused an embarrassingly overwhelming vulnerability—a condition of heart that I was much too familiar with as an adult.

Apparently, emotional handicaps can grow healthy roots, and mine had strengthened unseen and unattended, just waiting for droplets of water to urge the young shoots to ease up into the sunlight. To assimilate Dad's love, I needed to let it in gradually. But his letters came as a deluge.

He asked me to burn the letters in case Mom should ever find them. Given her unpredictable reaction to expressions of emotion or intimate conversation that excluded her, the fallout would've been disastrous. Still, Dad's request seemed ludicrous and magnified the secretive nature of our new relationship. He also requested that we establish a buffer zone of confidentiality. He didn't want me to share his private thoughts with anyone, and he would do the same for me. The secrecy felt seedy, as if we were having an affair.

When I spoke with my father on the phone, I kept my voice cool. I didn't want to hurt him, yet I wasn't ready to appear vulnerable in front of him. The unspoken closeness we once shared, so cherished by me as a child, seemed irretrievable and painfully elusive to me as an adult.

Despite my lack of encouragement, he was eager to dialogue about anything and was unyielding in his efforts to draw me out. I closed off even more. He claimed responsibility for my aloofness, saying that I learned my behavior from watching how he lived his life: how he turned away from his spouse, how he sequestered himself in the den every evening, how he distanced himself from his family. Of all the words he'd given me in his "love letters," these hit me the hardest. I'd always been proud of being like Dad, but I hadn't realized that I'd inherited not only his love of music and a quiet, internalized way of living—I'd inherited his emotional detachment too.

His first visit since the onset of the letters terrified me. Even though I was expecting him, the knock at my door made me flinch. When I let him in, he drew me into his arms and against his trembling body. The hug left moisture on my neck. He seemed like a dam crumbling under unbearable pressure.

My father's embrace was so potent that the imprint of his physical presence became a permanent memory felt on my arms and around my back. His energy flowed through me like a tsunami, upending and rearranging my entire perception of "us." Long after he left my apartment that day, the elements in my life—the letters, Mom, my brothers, my future relationships—were charged with new significance. I could no longer ignore the emotional inadequacy sequestered in my heart. Isolation's refuge wasn't enough anymore. At the same time, I resented being forced to release *my* impending deluge of emotion that was sure to come.

Included in Dad's confessions was the corroboration of a story Mom once told me about how he was her second choice for a husband. The other man, whom she *truly* loved, was a pilot in WWII who was shot down and killed in action. Dad was a First Lieutenant in charge of the litter collection detail in the second wave at Normandy. He carried the wounded and the dead off the beach.

For the first time, I saw my father in terms of where he'd come from and the sacrifices and choices he'd made. Like his mother, Birdie, he'd given up a life in music for his family. Plus, he was devoted to a wife and kids who never fully returned his love.

But he was wrong. I loved him with everything I was and ever would be.

The Rape

I woke up frozen with terror. I pulled the blankets up to my chin. The cries were close. Definitely not ten stories below on Broadway. They were coming from somewhere in my building.

The woman screamed again, and my body stiffened. I stopped breathing and stared out the window at the dense, sickening, brown fog. I felt like barfing. I pulled the phone into bed with me and dialed 911. The force of the screams was urgent and pushed like a knee into my chest. Clutching my robe, I got up and poked my head out into the hallway. The screams intensified.

"Help me! Someone help! Please stop! No . . . God, no! HELP!"

My heart lurched. I knew who was under attack. It was the jazz singer who lived in the last apartment on my side of the hall. Her screams were shredding the silky, expressive voice in her throat.

The screams kept coming. Why didn't the attacker cover her mouth? Where were the neighbors? The cops? I thought about knocking on her door and running away just to distract him, to buy time until help came. But I thought the guy might have a knife or a gun. I slunk partway down the hall and the screaming stopped. I felt dizzy. It was stupid to be in the hallway by myself. There was nowhere to hide. The thick carpet masked my footfalls as I rushed back to my apartment and locked the door. My hands were shaking. When the wails started up again, I stared into the stagnant brown fog and moaned. I wrapped my arms around myself and rocked side-to-side. I couldn't help imagining the worst.

I heard the muted "ding" of the elevator and the doors slid open. Commotion in the hall—guys in heavy boots—more screaming. I drew the covers over my head, but I kept listening. Suddenly, it sounded like a bomb had gone off. They must've rammed in the door. My chest heaved from taking in lungfuls of stale air. No matter how hard I squeezed my eyes shut, I couldn't dispel images of what they must've found inside.

Other than hearing that the jazz singer had been escorted out of the building by the EMTs, I never found out what happened to her. But after a few days, the police tape was gone and the boarded up apartment had a new door and a new tenant.

Vantage Point Shifted

Dad came for a visit the next day. I didn't tell him about the attack, but this time, his "hug of vulnerability" didn't make me squirm. I relaxed into his arms, and I was sure he felt the change. He never pushed for an explanation, but lines, like multiple horizons, stretched across his forehead for the rest of the visit.

My introverted and distant father had reinvented himself and our relationship. I was ready to do the same and vowed to myself that I would verbally reveal my true feelings on our next visit.

The following week, Dad had his first heart attack. The weight of my father's fragility debilitated me. For hours, I sat with my head in my hands and wept. My mind was plagued by the possibility of his death and I begged the gods for more time. I had no desire or discipline to sit at the piano and practice.

By the time he recovered, I found that my icy core had melted. But I still couldn't get anything significant to travel from my lips to my father's ear. My feelings had finally formed into sentences, but I hadn't learned the skill to purge them from my mouth. It physically hurt to feel the words die on my lips. I would've said, "I adore you, Dad. I need you and can't imagine life without you."

I cherished my father's letters. I was relieved that I'd kept them. Then, becoming the last Rich to leave New York, I moved from Manhattan to Hingham, Massachusetts, on the South Shore of Boston, specifically to be near Dad and Mom who'd retired to Cape

Cod. But somehow during the move, the letters were misplaced. That loss, from which I never recovered, fueled a self-deprecating time in my life during which I stopped saving any significant mementos—including programs and recordings of my own performances. The punishment only served to untether myself from the richness of my musical heritage, as well as my personal accomplishments.

The letters were gone, but what remained was the intensity of my father's love.

In the end, the one-sided letters had softened my heart. If Dad had given up on me, if he'd taken my stoic silence at face value and stopped writing, I might never have learned that grand gestures of love *do* work.

Part Six

Carol Rich

Horowitz

The earthen aroma of the New England woods supplanted New York's ubiquitous stink: urine in the subway, body odor on the bus, perfume mixed with pickles in the deli, that unavoidable special blend of hot pretzels and sauerkraut on the street corners.

The three-hundred-year-old house in Hingham, Massachusetts, had four fireplaces, including a huge one in my bedroom. Deer and fox trotted by my studio window at The South Shore Conservatory of Music while my students played Clementi and Bach. When it snowed, I strapped on my cross-country skis and took in lungfuls of crisp ocean air on my way to work.

My students at the conservatory were mostly kids whose parents forced them to take piano lessons. One boy consistently came to my studio directly from the soccer field, where he'd show up with creased muddy music and a fresh odor that remained in my studio for the rest of the day. Half of his lesson time was spent de-fidgeting him.

There was Dawna—the only person I ever knew to have a true case of tone-deafness. She couldn't discern if pitches were higher or lower. I called her Dawna for weeks until I saw in print that her name was Donna. As an experiment, I recorded saying her name with and without the Boston accent, but she couldn't hear the difference.

One of my older kids, a junior in high school, had the awkward but common combination of a love for the piano and a lack of natural ability. His musical goal was to play the theme from Pink Panther. After two years of sonatinas and Bach Inventions, which he learned to tolerate, I finally plopped the music to Pink Panther down in front of him. "Play it on the recital next month," I said. "Wear a little pink." His playing wasn't perfect, but he made up for it by sporting a full-on, shiny, pink suit.

My most talented student at the conservatory was a boy who was awarded a full scholarship. He was excruciatingly shy, but when he played, his thin face shone. His hands were expressively "soft," but something was wrong. There were deep ridges, dips, and white blotches on his fingernails. He was seriously malnourished. Unlike most parents who dropped off their kids for an hour with their babysitter (me), the boy's mother had a quiet sense of awe as she stayed to observe her son's interaction with music. One day, she came to me in tears. Her son's scholarship had been withdrawn. She was a single parent and couldn't continue to pay the minimal, weekly fee that the school required of scholarship recipients. I told her not to worry, it would all work out. She held a moist hanky in her fist and smiled feebly. Clearly, music was a lifeline for both her and her son. I had to do something. I gave the director an ultimatum: reinstate my student or I'd walk. The boy returned at his regular time the following week.

Soon after that, a small envelope appeared on the piano in my teaching studio. It was from the parents of three well dressed, smiles-that-reveal-braces sisters. They had back-to-back-to-back lessons on Friday afternoons. Their schoolbags were always bursting with homework and healthy snacks.

The envelope contained the best present I'd ever received from a student, or from anyone really—a coveted stage-seat ticket to see Horowitz.

❧

My first-row onstage seat at Boston's Symphony Hall was about ten feet away from the master, upstage between his piano and the back wall, perfectly in line with the keyboard. There was nothing between me and Horowitz's hands, feet, face, and bowtie. My right arm grazed the heavy velvet theater rope where he entered and exited. It was the best seat ever in the entire history of recital-going.

It took place on Sunday, October 19, 1986 at 4 P.M., Horowitz's preferred day and time to perform. The program consisted of some of his most beloved repertoire: two Scarlatti Sonatas, an Adagio, Rondo, and Sonata by Mozart, two Scriabin Etudes, the Schumann *Arabesque,* a Schubert-Liszt transcription, Liszt's *Sonetto 104 del Petrarca,* ending with two Chopin Mazurkas and the B Minor Scherzo.

Horowitz fans are rabid, and hurricane-force applause erupted after every piece. But whenever he lifted his hands to the keyboard, silence fell so hard, so abruptly, it was as if the entire audience had dropped through a trap door. When it was time for the Scherzo, Horowitz conjured power, yearning, passion, and unearthly demonic beauty. Even in the most dramatic sections, his motions were compact and minimalist—no wasted movement whatsoever. The velvety-toned lyricism he coerced from the piano came from his heart; but technically, the breath-stopping tone came from a stealthy combination of his fingers' cushion-like pads, the controlled speed of his first joints, and his choice of fingerings, which favored the third and fourth fingers—the ones with the most generous flesh on the pads.

Afterwards, the applause was a steady push of deafening adoration. Smiling broadly, Horowitz bowed and bowed. It was as if he was asking, "Are you sure I played well enough for an encore?" It took half a dozen curtain calls before he threw up his hands, put his handkerchief to his quivering smile, and finally returned to the piano. Tossing the tails of his tux over the back of the piano bench, he glanced at *me.* He seemed to be deciding what to play. I thought he might actually ask my opinion. He tilted his head, raised his eyebrows, and shrugged. Then, he audibly exhaled and placed his handkerchief inside the piano. The settling of the audience sounded like swans' wings folding at dusk.

Horowitz's tone and dazzling technique were why fans clamored for tickets, but the encores were what they flocked to hear. Which of his renowned chestnuts would he play? Would it be slow and soulful or sparkling and speedy? A two-minute gem or a five-minute *tour de force*? Horowitz lifted his left hand over the keyboard to prepare for, what I hoped would be, the first of many encores. Brushing a piece of red lint off the keys, he waited for the hush of the audience. Then his right hand floated up and he presented us with a gift of love—his trademark encore, Schumann's *Träumerei,* from *Kinderszenen,* "Scenes from Childhood." His programming was so generous, his touch so dear, his heart so on his sleeve—my every possible desire was met. His commitment to beauty, and to sharing beauty, was inspirational. Tears streamed down my cheeks. I couldn't brush them away, I couldn't breathe, I couldn't move. The audience was possessed too, and they just wouldn't let him quit. Horowitz didn't walk off before playing his next selection, Moszkowski's *Étincelles.* It was fast and clean—as if shooting stars got loose from the piano and sped around the hall like fireballs depositing sparkling silver light in their wake.

He held his hands to his heart as he bowed to the audience and then he turned around and bowed to the people in the stage seats. Looking me directly in the eye, he said, "I cannot play anymore." His English was heavily flavored with a Russian accent. He flaunted his famous smile, skipped his fingers up my forearm that rested on the rope, and left for good.

A few short years after Horowitz's passing, his Steinway went on tour. I thought it was amazing, but also kind of bizarre. When the Horowitz Steinway made a stop in Portland, I had it to myself for an entire hour. I played his repertoire, which by some grand fluke of three of my former teachers' designs, imitated my repertoire almost exactly. Touching the keys that Horowitz touched, playing the same repertoire—the same notes that he played—it was almost as if the Steinway knew how to negotiate the familiar passages without me. Envisioned tone corresponded exactly with the realized one. Everything in between, all the moving parts, piano and human, were conduits through which music passed. Just as he'd done in Boston, I ended with *Étincelles.*

I assume that before his passing, Horowitz consented to let his Steinway go on tour without him. Who else would understand the cravings of his admirers?

Nocturnality

I swallowed hard against the rising fright in my throat. Adrenalin was ravaging my nervous system and escape was crucial. I needed distance between me and my drenched bed sheets.

My rational brain was a sun-glassed woman, cigarette dangling from her nicotine-stained fingers, who searched the horizon while contemplating the idiocy of my terror. I gave her a cursory nod. She wasn't wrong.

Inside the car, I locked the door with my elbow, switched on the engine, pulled out the knob to the headlights, and rolled out of the driveway. The back of my neck tingled. The presence of the nocturnal lurker hovered high over the cobalt blue roof of my Datsun as I covertly coasted down the deserted streets of Hingham. Once past the city limits, I stepped on the gas. Even though the rearview mirror revealed only darkness, I knew that late-Autumn leaves churned up in my wake. Beneath my sweatshirt, my clothing clung to me like slimy endometrial lining.

As I drove, the self-loathing center in my brain played back the movie of my escape.

Something woke me up—probably the innocuous rustling of the tree by my window or headlights flickering across the ceiling. My heart thumped against my chest. In an effort to find a level horizon past the curtains, I propped up on one elbow. Flinging off the covers, I peered into the darkness as my pulse rocked my body. I threw on the sweatshirt and sneakers I kept at the foot of my bed, slunk past the closed doors of two sleeping roommates, sidestepped the creaky parts on the staircase, grabbed the car keys, and fled.

My fingers tightened around the steering wheel. The headlights floodlit shadows by the side of the wooded road. I slowed and made out a doe and her fawn, jaws askew with grass poking out between large, buck-toothed grins. Their glassy eyes followed me as I rolled past. Sweat dripped down between my shoulder blades, and when I cracked the window, the frigid air soothed my nerves. But relief was fleeting. A shiver seized my body. I left the window open and turned up the heat.

The nocturnal lurker never traveled far from my bed, and my breathing eased as I approached the last tight turns before reaching the spot where Massachusetts Bay joined the far reaches of Boston Harbor. I pulled into one of the three vacant bay-facing parking spots. The picture windows of the Cohasset estates up on the bluff were glazed over with the reflection of over-the-water nothingness. Spasm remnants seized my body. Cutting the engine, I slumped down under a blanket I kept in the back seat. Golden haze blurred the glowing beacons of boats and buoys in the bay, and water, black and slick as crow feathers, roiled up onto the rocky coastline like fingers aimlessly wandering—searching for familiar harmonies.

The intensity of the spasms decreased over time, and I sank into a blissful state of stasis. From my mind's faraway shores, the slow movement of Bach's Double Violin Concerto resonated in sweet-tempered echolalia. It was the kind of Bach that yearned for nothing. Except to simply . . . be.

Eye of the Storm

My New England life included a friendship-turned-affair with a heterosexual married woman. We rendezvoused at World's End, a coastal habitat area with a stunning view of the Boston skyline, fifteen miles across the water. Gentle breezes swirled around our mouths and tickled our necks as we reclined on a leaf-strewn hillside and read aloud to one another: Robert Frost, Rainer Maria Rilke, and Alice Walker's *The Color Purple.* The affair ended in the middle of the night with sounds of a ladder, the away-at-a-conference husband entering through a window, and my naked lover being punched and dragged to the floor.

The following week, my father died. The first person I called after regaining the ability to breathe was my only friend, the married woman, who hung up on me after a frosty, "There's no one here by that name."

It was only a one-hour drive to Cape Cod, where my parents were to live out their lives in a house they had built on a woodsy lot overlooking a cranberry bog. Four brief retirement years passed, and then, while taking his morning dog walk around the bog, Dad suffered a second heart attack. I was by his side in the I.C.U. the day before he died. His last words to me were, "Keep busy. I love you, Carol."

It was over a year before I could talk about him or listen to music without crying. The waves of grief gradually lessened, but they never fully left. When the fresh intensity of grief swells in my chest, I cling to it like lost love letters found.

A month after my father's funeral, hurricane Gloria made landfall over World's End and the entire eastern seaboard, all of which was expected to be inundated with seawater. Hingham was one town inland. I x-ed over the windows with masking tape, and stocked up on bottled water, non-perishables, and candles. My roommates were away, so it was just me crouched down under the kitchen table with my pillows, blankets, battery-powered lantern, and a book, which, due to nervousness and hurricane curiosity, remained unread until the next day.

It started with a few heavy raindrops, but then, the sky darkened, the power went out, and Gloria steam-rolled over my world. By noon, it was dark as night. The house shook and groaned. The biggest gusts sounded like jet planes crashing through the roof. The wind never stopped to breathe—it was one prolonged push.

Hours later, it ceased. No howling wind, no creaking walls, no branches scraping at the windows. It was the eye of the storm, and I wasn't prepared for it. After my hand's momentary hesitation on the doorknob, I pulled open the front door. My mind's black and white version of the hurricane's wrath was replaced with rich, rain-soaked greens and browns, and the sky was a cartoonish Ektachrome Blue. There wasn't a whisper of wind, not even a breeze. Uprooted centuries-old trees lay tossed to the ground, and one of the giant oaks lining the street had fallen neatly alongside my house. Its exposed root system was as tall as an African elephant.

We—the surviving trees, the house, and me—were only halfway through the storm. The second act roiled ominously on the horizon. Twenty minutes later, a gentle breeze quickly turned into a squall. I did a check of the house. The power was still out, but all the windows were intact. Branches from a fallen giant leaned precariously against one of the second story windows in my bedroom. I added extra tape to keep the glass intact in case the next round of hurricane winds pushed the tree limb through.

Being outside, in the eye, had given me hope. I'd be okay. Gloria howled and complained until nightfall, when it unwound into a typical autumn rainstorm.

As always in October, the landlord had provided a healthy stack of wood for the fireplaces. It was now my sole source of warmth, and after two days without power, I started to conserve. I slept, ate, and read by the fireplace in the living room instead of igniting the one in my bedroom every night. Donning my fingerless gloves, I spent long hours practicing by candlelight. After five days without power, I became an expert fireplace cook. Baked potatoes were the best, but even canned soup was satisfying after being heated by the edges of the fire. My perishables were gone, but I'd taken the warnings to heart. I'd stocked up on plenty of food: baked beans, rice, canned chili, and of course, tea and coffee. After a week without power, I enjoyed life lit by fire and candlelight. I had a candle setup in every room. It was cozy, and I thrived. The aroma of wood smoke permeated the darkest corners of the house—the places where firelight couldn't reach.

One day, I heard the whirring, grinding sounds of chain saws and wood chippers. Then, after ten days without power, the lights came on. It was so jarring, so unpleasant—I immediately shut them off. Every trace of mood and solitude in my candle-lit life had been swallowed up by electric light. When the heat kicked on and the fridge started up, it was time to bid Gloria farewell.

Part Seven

The Glance

It was a glance the likes of which only a fish could give: a flat-headed sideways blank stare. I squatted at the river's edge and opened my hand. The fish flipped its tail against my palm and plopped back into the glistening water. Hopefully, for the fish, the only memory of me would be as something to push against. I held my breath as it darted through the current. It seemed okay, but I knew it would never be the same.

I stood on the rocky beach and listened to the gurgle of the river. It was November of 1988, and having just moved from New England to the Pacific Northwest, I was determined to start my new life by finding a better way to commune with nature. I needed to spend more time simply being among.

Blimp House Barn Owls

Lifting the heavy chain over my head, I squeezed in through an opening in the blimp house's massive doors. In the next second, my olfactory senses were assaulted by a wildly pungent odor, and I buried my nose in the crook of my arm. At first, I couldn't see to the end of the cavernous space, but as my eyes adjusted to the gloom, I made out the silhouettes of four small blimps tethered to the floor by the farthest wall. Countless dust motes floated weightlessly in filtered light streaming in from hundreds of small translucent windows near the ceiling.

Splotches of bird poop and large brown and white striped feathers plastered the dirt floor next to the wooden walls. The origin of the stench was solved, but I had yet to find the source of a mysterious shuffling sound. Lifting my gaze, I saw dozens of Barn Owls roosting in the rafters doing what owls do: cuddling, cooing, ruffling feathers, and plucking out the innards of voles and mice.

The owls' detached acceptance of my presence overrode my feelings of intrusion, and soon, my olfactory senses accepted the wild, pungent atmosphere.

Two years later, in 1992, the blimp house's twin structure burned down. Left behind were two titanic steel frames where wooden doors once hung. The surviving structure, the Barn Owl blimp house, originally a WWII military blimp hangar on the Oregon Coast, had been transformed into the Tillamook Air Museum. There wasn't any sign of owls the day I waited on line to pay $15 admittance. No poop, no feathers, no cooing, no wild odor—just glossy white paint, war planes hanging from the ceiling, and well-displayed photos of blimps from days of yore.

Still, the gentle echo of ruffling feathers stirred in the air like monks mouthing their prayers to a deaf god.

Carol Rich

The Ghost in Room 7

My teaching studio at the University of Portland was a windowless, cement-walled box in the basement of the music building. Regardless, it brought back fond memories of the "cells" at Hartt, which were perennially crawling with panicked instrumentalists and vocalists who crammed scales and Clementi Sonatinas into their brains and uncooperative hands in order to pass the piano proficiency exam. However, the professors at Hartt allowed piano majors to practice in the studios, classrooms, and performance halls. For whatever reason, U. of P. students didn't practice at night much, so even though I had a Steinway at home, I occasionally stayed late to take advantage of the unique isolation in my studio-cell.

I was reworking Scriabin's Ninth Sonata, the *Black Mass.* The 4' 10" Russian composer was a self-proclaimed mystic who believed that his music was a portal to the preternatural. As you'd expect, the *Black Mass* is spooky and disturbing.

Initially, deciphering the score had taken countless hours of intense, concentrated study simply to be able to stumble through. That phase was years behind me, and it was time to create a viable interpretation that would marry divine wisps of evocative harmonies with brutally driven climaxes charged with multiple finger and arm trills, tremolos, grueling passagework, and loin-girding crescendos. It would require the utmost physical and mental endurance.

I breathed deeply and my body relaxed. Isolation was complete. I gave the opening five-note melody to the night. Time passed as the theme wended through the sonata.

Suddenly, the music was bounding mercilessly across treacherous terrain, aiming directly toward a cliff. Hurling itself over the edge, the music's momentum suddenly seized up and the ground dropped away, leaving the insidiously creeping, five-note melody floating midair. My body sizzled as my arms hovered over the keyboard. My heart pounded. In that moment, retaining control was like driving straight on black ice.

Despite the lingering shot of adrenalin, my fingertips remained on the surface of the keys, where they slunk along with minimal movement. Maintaining stillness, I prepared for the last terrifying outburst. A growl rumbled inside the piano, and primal power propelled my arms as I launched into the final episode. . . .

Screeech! My hands jumped off the keys, and I held my breath. I listened. The sudden jolt of sound had occurred in conjunction with my own cacophony, but it was on the other side of the door. Sliding off the piano bench, I inched the door open. An elongated square of sickening yellow light sprang onto the green carpet in front of my studio. "It's just the light from your room, idiot," I mumbled. The basement was dark, including the ten small practice rooms around the perimeter of the lounge. As usual, the doors were left open—all except for one—the door to room 7. A window in the door revealed that the light was off in there too. I wiped my clammy hands on my pants.

I turned to go back to my cement box. *Screeech!* There it was again, this time without the distraction of Scriabin's apocalypse. The noise definitely came from room 7. It was the unmistakable scrape of a piano bench being dragged across a cement floor. A spasm gripped my stomach. Most likely, there was a student sitting in the dark getting in touch with their *angst.* I considered grabbing my stuff and getting the heck out of there, but I needed to know what, or who, made the noise.

Turning on the overhead lights in the lounge, I checked the other rooms with open doors. No one was there. All that was left was room 7. I put my hand on the doorknob and flung the door into the room, where it ricocheted off the inside wall. Cold air hit my face and crept around my neck. I walked my fingers along the wall and flipped the switch, flooding the room with stark white light. I imagined my pupils suddenly constricting. The room was empty, but the bench *had* been pushed back away from the piano. "I hope you enjoyed the Scriabin," I said. Then I shut off the light.

Something in the air shifted. My skin tingled. I struggled to breathe. I sprinted the few yards to my studio, shoved my music in my bag, and bolted up the stairs to the main lobby, where the air was only slightly less oppressive. I could see through the tall glass windows to my car, which sat under a lamppost in the parking lot. It must've been close to midnight, and I was surprised to see two other cars parked next to mine.

Music was coming from the performance hall. I wasn't aware of other people in the building, and I felt obliged to warn them about the ghost, or whatever it was, in the basement. I went through the backstage entrance, where I found the guitar teacher giving a lesson to a bloodshot-eyed young man. They looked up and the teacher let out a sigh.

He said, "Oh, it's you. We've been hearing things."

"Me too. What kinds of things?"

"Bumping, there behind the curtain. No one's there. We looked. Was it you?"

"No. There's something downstairs too."

The air was getting thicker. My throat felt like it was in a vice.

"I'm getting out of here," I said.

The teacher peered over the top of his glasses. "Wait up. Let's go together. We're done." The student's guitar was already in the case.

Seconds later, I was reveling in the freshness of the night.

Shenanigans on the Catwalk

I'd just gotten up from the piano when there was a huge crash on stage directly behind me. Running toward the wings, I was instantly engulfed in a cloud of thick dust that billowed out from the blast. Several friends in the choir rushed into the cloud to save me.

"I'm over here. I'm okay!" I said.

My near-demise had occurred during a dress rehearsal with Choral Cross-ties, at George Fox University, about forty-five minutes outside of Portland. Since the piece was *a cappella,* without accompaniment, and the choir was so exceptional and well prepared, I'd gotten up from the piano to go out to the seats and listen.

After the dust had settled, I could see that a steel counterweight about the size of a door had broken loose from above, splintered my piano bench, and left a trench in the stage. The piano was untouched, but both it and my performance blacks would need a thorough cleaning inside and out.

That night, on a whim, I went to a theme party called "The Ghosts of Oregon." I didn't think much about the subject matter until I randomly picked up one of the ghost-related books piled up on a coffee table. The yellowed pages flipped open to a chapter titled, "The Ghosts of George Fox University." At first, I thought someone in the choir rigged the book so it would open to that page, but there weren't any choir members there. I chuckled to myself, but my stomach was in my throat. I couldn't resist reading the story about a "mischievous ghost" who hangs around the music building and plays pranks on people. It was known to haunt the catwalk over the stage.

A few years later, I returned to George Fox to accompany a tenor recital. Of course, the dent in the stage had been repaired, but my memory of having escaped death-by-crushing-counterweight was still fresh. I glared at the catwalk overhead.

The recital progressed as usual until the last song before intermission. The tenor had sung his last phrase and I was playing the postlude, an extended piano solo at the end of the piece. Every nerve in my body was on alert as I anticipated a rousing finish to the first half of the program. Injecting the music with maximum energy, I intensified my focus on the last measure, still two lines away. It felt like I was running on high-octane as I executed the final phrase of passagework.

Suddenly, as if on cue, when my hands came down on the last chord, one of the piano legs gave way and the 9-foot Steinway crashed to the deck. The piano landed at a severe angle, but I'd pulled my legs out just in time. Once again, my performance blacks were covered in dust. The tenor gracefully hopped away from the piano, and we gawked at one another in disbelief. He'd been in the choir the day the counterweight had come crashing down, and I'm sure he was having the same flashback.

I threw up my hands. I had no control over the resounding clangor that emerged from the bowels of the piano. A few seconds passed before the befuddled audience rose to its feet and let out a roar of applause, peppered with expletives. We took our bows, and I motioned to the piano for its unparalleled contribution to an unforgettable half-recital.

Part Eight

Carol Rich

Finding Georgia

It was 1993. I'd been in Oregon for five years, but instead of cultivating friends, most of my time and energy had been squandered crowbarring my way out of my ex's family. Finally, after my hard-fought liberation, I sought out the company of other musicians, but the ease of friendship I'd experienced in New York, West Hartford, and Boston, eluded me in Portland. After performances, the symphony and ballet musicians flocked together like pelicans circling and flapping while their pouches teemed with fish. I was a lone loon floating on dark water.

Then one day, Laurel, my cat-figurine-in-every-corner, bubbly-yet-depressed neighbor, sent me an invitation to a wine and tarot party. I accepted. I considered the party a lark, something quirky to lure me away from practicing—a way to be among people.

When it was my turn, I slid back the silk curtain and placed a twenty dollar bill beneath a slinking, butt-raised, black cat figurine paperweight. The room reeked of perfume. On the table sat a regular deck of cards, not the tarot deck I expected. Bonnie, the card reader, flipped over an eight of clubs.

"You have two brothers. One of them is named Ken."

Two more cards went onto the pile: the three of diamonds and the king of spades. She glanced at me over the top of her white, sparkly glasses. An eyebrow arched.

"This is good. You'll meet someone who will make up for the wrongs of your previous relationship. This person will be fair skinned with light hair and blue eyes. You'll meet at work. Soon."

A glimmer in Bonnie's eyes made me squirm. She knew Ken's name. Did she know about my ex's promiscuous, lying, teenage daughter from whom I'd had to safeguard even my underwear under lock and key? Did she know about the charming, yet criminal teenage son who'd gotten drunk and driven a stolen car onto someone's lawn where he smashed a rival's nose with the cast on his broken arm?

Bonnie grinned, scooped up the cards, and lifted a glass of red wine to her heavily lip-sticked mouth. She fussed with her haystack of bleached blonde hair. My reading lasted all of a minute. I thought, "How am I supposed to find the love of my life at the ballet? They're mostly gay guys and ballerinas. I'm doomed."

A week later, I was in the dance studio playing the piano reduction of *The Nutcracker.* In walked the stage manager and Georgia, the new assistant stage manager. At the break, I went to say hi. She was, after all, a lesbian-sister. I'd been wearing my piano glasses, and from across the room, I'd missed the cute smile, shiny strawberry-blond hair, and mischievous blue eyes that wended a quick path to my heart. I was smitten.

After having played hundreds of Nutcrackers in years past, the ballet took on new meaning after that. Georgia and I squeezed in dates between shows.

One time, during intermission, I found her sitting at her station in the production office.

"Hey," she said. "How's it going in the pit?"

"Fine. It's dark." My face flushed. I touched her shoulder and her hand found mine. The lighting designer and his assistant glanced up from their work.

Georgia mouthed the words, "Want to go to a movie?"

When she picked me up in her Volkswagen van, I gripped the handhold, and playfully hoisted myself up onto the squeaky seat. I gazed out over the world. I liked it. Our first official date was to a

"Livingroom Theater," where we snuggled against each other and watched a neoprene-clad Meryl Streep defend her family while she paddled down a white-water river. Afterwards, a cool breeze fluttered around our mouths as Georgia leaned down and softly kissed me on the lips. She cooked tofu sandwiches for me, and in the mornings, she smiled and laughed as she scrambled up the best eggs and veggie bacon I'd ever had. There were twenty-six Nutcrackers that month, and we spent our only day off together—Christmas Day. We went to the Oregon Coast, where Georgia reserved a cozy room equipped with an in-room hot tub and fluffy matching bathrobes. "It's not right on the beach," she said. "But I promise you'll like it." Did I ever.

I stripped off my sweaty performance blacks and pulled on jeans and a lightweight sweater. The feel of street clothes and sneakers made me happy. Flipping off the light in my dressing room, I bounded down the stairs and headed to the loading dock for some fresh air. A full moon hung in the crevasse-like space between Portland's downtown buildings. I replayed the performance in my mind; my onstage solo with the dancers went well. I was doing what I loved, I lived in a great city, and I was in a wonderful relationship.

Then Georgia, who'd briefly, uncharacteristically, snuck away from her stagehand duties, appeared and asked if I wanted to elope after the reset for the next day's performance. "Heck, yeah," I said. We'd been hoping for a (not-yet-legal) "wedding" with friends looking on, but we couldn't get them to agree on a date. Eloping was the perfect solution.

It was almost midnight by the time we picked up our rings at a friend's place and swung by the house to pick up Georgia's dog/witness, Wyler. We drove to Crown Point in the Columbia Gorge, where we said a few ceremoniously romantic words to one another. It was in the days before there was a visitor center and museum in the historic Vista House, our lofty elopement spot. In daylight, you can see eagles and ospreys soar through the vastness that defines the gorge. At night, it was all pinpoints of light on the Columbia, and lots of isolation. The wind wasn't the only thing making my teeth rattle. We were saying vows, exchanging rings, kissing.

A few years later, in 2004, we were officially married the day . . . no . . . the hour it became legal in Oregon. The historical mass wedding occurred in the same venue as the ballet I was playing at the time—my dressing room was upstairs on the third floor. Georgia's and my stagehand friends joined us to act as our witnesses.

We did the traditional cake tasting. Holy shit—yum! "That's why people make such a fuss over this stuff," we said. We registered at Target, and Crate and Barrel. There was a blowout party, and then we settled into officially being wife and wife. When we got a refund check in the mail, we learned that the marriage was never acknowledged in the eyes of the law.

Two years after that, we went north to Vancouver, B. C., where same-sex marriage was commonplace. "At least we'll be married in an entire country," said Georgia. Six of our friends made the trip over the border to watch us say another set of vows, this time, before a Canadian magistrate. The wedding took place in Stanley Park, out in the open, in daylight, with our friends looking on. Married three times to the same woman, and never divorced.

Carol Rich

Snowy

Living in the Pacific Northwest had prompted my love of all things wild to grow into full-blown obsession. Matt Zaffino, a local meteorologist in Portland, Oregon, infused his segments with stories about aurora borealis sightings, the Rover's findings on Mars, the growing cone inside the crater of Mount St. Helens, and the latest whereabouts of wolf pups in Oregon and Washington. One night, Matt reported on a Snowy Owl irruption that occurs every four or five years. Snowy Owls fly south from the arctic so that food in their northern territories can replenish. Heading south allows snowy babies to fill up on lemmings and voles, their preferred food source.

I discovered online reports of Snowy Owl sightings on the Oregon and Washington coasts and at Ridgefield Wildlife Refuge, which was just thirty minutes away from home. The news was barely out of my mouth before Georgia was packing her binoculars and camera. We visited every recommended site, searched every field and outcropping of rocks. We endured coastal squalls and wind-strewn sand—but the snowies eluded us.

I checked the rare-bird sites daily, and learned that birders were flightier than their subjects. Understandably, in order to protect the location of a rare species, people encouraged secrecy. A few rare birders were more forthcoming. They'd spotted Snowy Owls near the Washington coast and posted directions to the exact location. It was a long drive for a daytrip, but it would be worth it if we got to see even one owl.

❧

We pulled into a sandy parking spot by a spit of land that arched out ten miles into the Pacific. The owls were out there somewhere. Supposedly, they were about two and a half miles down the spit. The walk on sand made the going slow; Georgia had bad knees and I had a bad back, but slow still gets you there. Snow-covered mountain ranges skirted every horizon out of which rose a vibrant blue sky. There were plenty of potential avian distractions: bulbous-billed scoters, hovering terns, and flocks of darting sandpipers. Gigantic tree trunks were strewn about on the sand, most likely deposited there by the lethal combination of hurricane winds and high surf. No doubt, the severed trunks were once members of an old growth forest. Georgia fit neatly inside the biggest specimen.

We spotted a broken line of beach hikers who looked like ants going up and down the spit. My confidence was high. People were smiling and giving us the thumbs up. They'd seen the owls. The main ant line went up the spit all the way to the horizon, but several individuals fanned out to the left, away from the beach. I had no idea what sort of terrain Snowy Owls preferred: trees, the ground, the beach, a stump. There were so many places where a creature could hide. Scanning the reeds for white owl heads, I also kept an eye out for a fox or coyote. With owls and lemmings in the neighborhood, it seemed plausible that larger predators would be around.

When we reached the spot where people had fanned out, the beach opened up onto an area overlaid with grasses, stumps, and shrubs. Fallen trees, pale gray on white sand, lay weather-beaten and tossed into piles where creatures could hide. The relentless wind wended through the fabric of my coat. My teeth rattled. But we knew we were close when we saw a dozen people posed, frozen mid-step—awkward bipeds respectfully trying to blend in. Birders. The only sounds were the wind and an occasional cry from a gull. We took one of the multiple follow-me-to-nowhere trails and joined the hopeful. I focused my attention on a stand of tall sun-faded grass clumps that would be the perfect hiding place for a large white bird.

Georgia was doing a slow-motion dance. Flashing a wide-eyed look, she pointed to a spot in the field. It took me a few seconds to look beyond the obvious dunes, windblown grass, and beached tree limbs. Then I saw it—a smallish Snowy Owl sitting on a sun-bleached stump. Its head moved like you'd expect, swiveling side to side as it kept track of a handful of stealthy birders. I lifted my camera and snapped a few shots. I approached the owl in shifts, like in the children's game, "Mother, May I?" As I advanced at intervals of ten feet or so, I kept clicking away until I was close enough to tiptoe forward two feet at a time. There was no ruffling of wings, no shifting of feet, no sidewise glances at a perch farther away. I was being granted nearness.

We found nine Snowy Owls that day. Several of them were perched on logs as they scanned the fields. A few soared low near the shore while turning their heads this way and that. I'd never seen a bird so blatantly fly one way and look the other. Others, like the original one, sat on stumps or hillocks. Most had their glowing eyes half closed, as if napping while alert. As you'd expect, Snowy Owl feathers are pure white, but up close, you can see that the female adult owls' backs and heads have bars of dark stitching. Snowies' faces are covered in wispy, white feathers that flutter in the wind, and they exhibit permanent grins, as if they possess inside information. Unlike most birds, they're not afraid of eye contact, and they know how to use it. Their gaze is shockingly humanlike—intense and unwavering. Or perhaps, human gazes are shockingly owlish.

I jumped when Georgia's cool fingers entwined with mine. A Snowy Owl's keen golden eyes took us in. Sitting on a weatherworn tree limb, its white owl body stood out against the vibrant blue sky.

Black and Red—Xen and Zoe

Two other names were on the list ahead of mine. I paced and waited for the doors to open. Forty-five minutes later, the key turned in the latch and a small throng of people pushed into the waiting room ahead of me. I sat across from a painting of a dog that looked like my sweet Scarbo, who died two months ago, just prior to the death of our other elderly dog, Chonka. I swallowed against the lump in my throat.

Boisterous people filled every corner of the room, but families with kids and dogs were the loudest. My heart sank. "Of course they'll get first dibs," I thought. Chances of the staff adhering to the list seemed unlikely. But then, the first name was called and a grizzled farmer stepped up to the counter. He flipped the pages of the photo album until he stopped to point to a spot on one of the pages. His lips trembled with a smile. He pushed the palms of his hands to his bloodshot eyes. One of the workers, a dreadlocked young woman, placed her hand on the man's arm.

"I'll bring him to room one, over there, okay? It'll just take a minute."

The man scratched the bristles on his cheek. "My son's coming too."

"Good. I'll show him where you are."

The second name on the list was called, and a woman with two girls stepped up to the counter. The younger girl picked her nose.

Her older sister slapped the goober onto the floor. When the mother pointed to a photo in the album, the dreadlocked woman smiled. "She's a cutie. I didn't think she'd be here long, just came in yesterday. We'll bring her to room two."

A dreadlocked, tattooed man came from the back, leading a black and white, longhaired, gray-muzzled dog.

"Room one," said the woman at the counter. "Companion dog."

"Perfect," said the man.

A third dreadlocked worker came out from the back, carrying an adorable longhaired dachshund puppy.

"Room two."

"Good luck, puppy," I thought.

When my name was called, I stepped up to the book and found the photos I'd seen online of five lab puppy siblings. According to the information on the no-kill shelter's website, they were prematurely abandoned by their mom. I put my hand on the photos of the reddish/yellow puppy and one of the black puppies.

The woman's face glowed. "You want to see two? That's great."

"Yep. Both girls, right?"

"Uh huh. The other black one's a female too. The chocolate and the mottled are boys. They're all lab mixes. They came in a few days ago, but except for the chocolate, they were really small and still transitioning to kibble. This is their first day to be seen. We'll bring your *two* to room one: black and red sisters. I believe the other dog from room one is already adopted."

The grizzled man's son was filling out forms in the outtake area. Next to the paperwork sat the parting gifts: bags of treats, food, poop bags, toys, vet coupons, etc. His father sat bent over his new companion, the eight-year-old black and white spaniel. His gnarled fingers stroked the soft fur and found the place behind its ears that made the dog look up as he leaned into the man's legs.

Room one was littered with squeaky toys, plush toys, a tennis ball, two chairs, and paper towels. I couldn't believe Georgia trusted me to pick out a puppy for her, but she'd committed to teaching a scuba class in Puget Sound. Waiting for a time when we could both go would mean that someone else would snatch up the puppies we wanted. It was up to me. "Pick out one of the black females," she'd said.

I jumped when the door opened. The dreadlocked woman entered holding two puppies. They were much smaller than I anticipated, four and a half pounds each. Their tiny legs reached for me as she placed them in my arms. I smelled their sweet puppy breath as they licked each other's eyes and then licked the salty trickles of water on my face. Their warm furry bodies vibrated against my chest.

"Poke your head out when you're done. Take your time." The woman smiled and closed the door.

The puppies squirmed, and my hands cupped their bald tummies as I lowered them to the floor. They immediately took off in a yippy, jumpy game of tag. The puppies were no match for the slippery floor, and their attempts to tear across the room ended in a pile of legs, noses, and tails. The black one, who had dabs of white on her toes, chest, and the tip of her tail, found the plush toys first, but she quickly snubbed them and stepped up to the tennis ball. Her nose was level with the top of it. She touched it with her paw and when the ball wobbled, she reared up on her hind legs and toppled over. Wrinkles appeared on the forehead of the red puppy, but her bitsy tail was wagging. She pounced on her sister and they rumbled around my legs. Then suddenly, as only puppies can, they plopped down on my sneakers and fell asleep. An entire five seconds passed before little squeaks came from their yawning mouths. The pink of their tiny tongues reminded me of Bazooka Joe bubble gum. Blinking sleepy puppy eyes looked up at me, and the red puppy reached up with her paws. Like her sister, there was a brushstroke of white on her chest. I gathered them both into my arms and kissed their soft faces.

The outtake area was filled with the newly adopted. The long-haired dachshund puppy was going home with the two girls, and the chocolate lab puppy was there too. He was a big boy—about the size of his two sisters combined. He sat contemplatively on the lap of a serious young man who was waiting to take him home.

My puppies had room to spare in the towel-lined cat carrier I'd stowed in the back of the Smart Car. They were content, curious, relaxed passengers. I couldn't wait for Georgia to meet them. I adjusted the rearview mirror so I could watch their exceptional cuteness on the way home.

Then the sun hit the fur on Georgia's black dog. It was tinged with brown. I felt sick. "Should I go back and change it out for the other black female?" I thought. I'd fallen hard for both puppies. They loved each other, and they loved me. I gripped the steering wheel and sobbed. The pups tilted their heads as they looked at me through the slats of the carrier.

They were thinking, "What's wrong, Mommy?" God, they were already calling me Mommy.

I tried multiple times to reach Georgia, but she was probably underwater. I made a U-turn. Then the phone rang. I pulled over.

"Honey, your dog's brown. It was black until the sun hit it. I'm on my way back to . . ." I choked on the last words.

"What? Is it cute?"

"So cute."

"Do you love it?"

"Of course."

"Keep her, silly. I'm sure I'll love her. Turn the car around. Take them home."

"Really? Okay. Come home soon."

As promised, Georgia loved her puppy the second she snuggled it up to her beautiful face.

Zoe became my soulmate.

The O

The topic is uncontainable, a rabbit hole, a mirror, a long and hearty hike to the heart. The Piano. Has the centuries-old wood of my lifelong companion absorbed my energy—my chi? Does it recognize my touch as I depress the keys to extract its most luscious tone? Has some essence of my piano's wood, which was harvested in 1903, migrated into me through vibrational osmosis? Caring for my aging Steinway is uncomplicated, straightforward. When it complains, parts are replaced, reshaped, retuned, micro-measured, and cleaned. Presto! Its life is extended.

I know its every curve, every nuance of shading in the rare wood. I know the origins of every scratch inflicted upon its longsuffering body. The marks in the fallboard were passionately inflicted by swift swipes of fingernails in the heat of music-making. People ask why I don't replace the heavily scarred fallboard. They say that the original gold filigree Steinway insignia can be replaced with a new updated one. But the marks reveal decades of devotion—they're epochs of a tree's life marked off in rings. They're wrinkles on my beloved's face.

My teaching career began in tenth grade, and by the time I was a senior, I'd made enough money to buy a used burgundy Mustang fastback. It was probably the coolest thing I'd ever do. I gave lessons at the high school, but other than that, and a brief stint going house to house, my teaching life had occurred in colleges, conservatories, and private studio spaces. When I hit my mid-fifties, I wanted to teach out of my home, and for the first time, I'd be sharing my Steinway with my students. However, it was on the verge of being a P. S. O., a Piano Shaped Object. Throughout the years, I'd done my best to replace hammers, pins and strings, but it was never student-worthy. *I* was content with its crazy bright sound, but I knew about tone production and how to create a *pianississimo* dynamic on the most difficult instruments. It made playing on the 9-footers in the concert halls that much more gratifying. Getting a partial result on an imperfect piano didn't insult my sensibilities. Students would, and should, be fussier. Teaching tone and control on the piano the way it was seemed unfair and subpar. Plus, I cringed when I imagined finesse-challenged students muscling their way through my piano's easy action by pounding out fistfuls of notes. Some people play as if they have jackhammers for hands—until someone firmly, lovingly, lifts their resistant arms from the keyboard.

For the first time ever, I considered selling my Steinway O and putting the money toward a new piano. I secretly confessed that creating gorgeous tone with minimal effort, and attaining a wider variety of nuance and tonal texture would be fun for me too—life changing, really. When I got to the piano dealership, I went straight to the Steinway Room. Then I laid my hands on a new Steinway B.

The cost was ridiculously prohibitive, but it was too late. I'd fallen in love. The piano responded to every subtlety, every whim, every soaring melody released from my heart.

I made out a sizable check for a deposit and my chest literally fluttered when the saleswoman placed a red notice on the music rack indicating that it was on hold for ten days pending final sale. It felt like I was buying a house. In fact, it cost almost as much as the house we'd bought fifteen years ago. Buying new shoes or performance blacks usually got me wound up, but the purchase of a new piano made my head swim. Once in the car, I gripped the steering wheel while fits of hysterical laughter took turns with waves of unbearable panic. Once the initial spew of emotions passed, I turned on the engine and pulled away.

Then I got home. Compared to the sleek matte black finish of the new piano, my 1913 Steinway looked worn and dejected. Even with the line of credit, I'd have to sell my baby to afford the new one. I looked at the marred Steinway insignia and played the Aria from the Goldberg Variations. Suddenly, I was weeping, falling to my knees. The thought of watching the movers take her out the front door ripped my heart to shreds. Bawling, I dropped to the floor and hugged one of the piano legs. I could never let her go.

I called the piano store and cancelled the deal. That too broke my heart, but it was bearable. I'd lost nothing. It occurred to me that there might be a compromise, a way to upgrade and to keep my beloved piano. I invested in a rebuild.

It was a relief to get a much smaller loan. Plus, I purchased a new upright Baldwin I could use for concerto accompaniments and two-piano repertoire. The rebuild successfully brought fresh purpose to my elderly piano that received all new parts except for the original soundboard, keys, and of course, the fallboard.

Just between you and me, I often reminisce about my brief affair with that Steinway B.

Carol Rich

In Symphony

I'm upstage right, in my comfort zone behind the 9-foot Steinway. The contemporary piece, *Three Latin-American Dances for Orchestra,* by Gabriela Lena Frank, is well-written for the piano. It "lies under the hand" as well as most orchestral keyboard parts in the canon of big-name composers.

Through the years, I'd developed my personal favorites for each of the five keyboard instruments I was required to play: piano, celesta, harpsichord, organ, and electronic keyboard—often moving from instrument to instrument during one piece. They call this doubling, tripling, or quadrupling. Talk about thinking ahead!

On the piano, I loved the florid, bold nature of the solos in Stravinsky's *Firebird.* Some would say, "But Carol, what about *Petrouchka*?" As a kid, my pile of records from the N.Y. Public Library often included various renditions of *Petrouchka.* Its high joy content and crisp, innovative instrumentation placed it in my top ten back then. But performing it to an audience of 3,000 concertgoers was only truly fun a handful of times. I'm still waiting for the childlike joy to return, and I know it will, when I can listen to a recording of it without experiencing the forced excitement during the unruly piano solos.

I'd rather be playing Copland's *Appalachian Spring,* which is just as exposed, but in a good way—exhilarating and gratifying every time, especially the smaller, chamber version for 13 players, which was commissioned by Martha Graham.

For celesta, after hundreds of performances of *Danse de la Feé Dragée* (Dance of the Sugar Plum Fairy) from *The Nutcracker,* plus several hundred more while dreaming, I was fortunate never to have lost the newness, crispness, spookiness, and outright excitement of playing it to a packed house.

It went like this: The lights on stage shifted, and I listened to the hard toes of pointe shoes scattering off the stage above our heads. After a few seconds, it started with four measures of intro, the second two softer than the first: *Bum-pah, Bum-pah, Bum-pah, Bum-pah; bum-pah, bum-pah, bum-pah, bum-pah, bum* . . . You know the rest.

I'd keep my hands calmly alert in my lap for the first two measures; then, as if it was part of the choreography, I'd lift them into position over the E Minor chord that begins the Sugar Plum's solo. It was a habit I started early on that removed all possibility of entering too soon, while simultaneously allowing time to set my hands before safely launching into the famous solo.

There can be a fair amount of goofing around in the pit, and it takes discipline not to get distracted. Plus, playing so many repetitions of a piece encourages complacency—that's when truly mortifying accidents can happen. But it was easy to get caught up in the music. Tchaikovsky gave us a great score, with soaring themes, creative instrumentation, texturally rich counter-themes, and dazzling solos. There are valid reasons why popular pieces are beloved by loyal audiences and performers.

Near the end of my symphonic career, I was gifted the honor of playing celesta in Holst's *The Planets*. The 7th movement, *Neptune, the Mystic,* features a truly heavenly celesta part with its mischievously playful chords and swirling arpeggios. Holst must've added a sprinkling of celestial gold dust the day he wrote it. Having played only three rehearsals and three performances of it in my entire life, *Neptune* remains a musical highlight. *The Planets* was another "regular" in my stack of LPs when I was a kid, and the initial thrill of discovery shines even more vibrantly now. I cherished every moment of playing the celesta. It was like a cottage at the beach I looked forward to visiting every chance I got.

But, my true symphonic home would always be at the 9-foot Steinway, upstage right. It was my bubble of happiness and comfort. When we assembled several times a week, we orchestra musicians were like family—fleeting, yet substantial. My symphony sister, the harpist, sat downstage to my right, and was always ready with a quick quip and a wink. My rambunctious brothers (plus the occasional sister), the percussionists, stood upstage on the risers to my left—barricaded but never forgotten behind a wall of sound shields. The winds and brass filled out center stage; they were the fun aunts and uncles happily exhibiting their exceptional telepathic skills as they breathed, phrased, and balanced as one.

The violinists and violists, the distant cousins, spread out in front of me, resembling a field of swaying, sawing willows. Clear across the stage, the low strings carried the weight of our ancestors, always reminding us from whence our roots originated. The unique sound of strings-alone that comes from an orchestra is nothing one can imagine until heard live and in close proximity. All those bows being drawn across the strings with a unified speed and intensity sounds like wind blowing through a cavern, on top of which is carried tone—the collective human soul—the identifying core of the symphony orchestra.

The conductor, somewhere way the heck out there, was the godparent of the entire clan.

Being on stage amongst a fine symphony orchestra is thrilling. I miss being there, in the moment—taking it all in.

After many measures of rest, I prepare to join the pulsing Latin rhythms of Gabriela Lena Frank's piece. My hands are poised to play. Focusing on the conductor, I peripherally catch the timpanist glancing at me as he raises his mallets over the drums. After a cursory nod-cue from the conductor, the timpanist and I launch into a driving rhythm, propelling the energy forward. After a few measures, the thunder from the timpani fades away, leaving it all in my hands, which become powerful mountain lions bounding around the hills and valleys of the keyboard. The strings join in with a Latin American tune, while I continue with my triplet rhythm. My part is so beautifully written that the composer gifted me one free measure—a moment of preparation—before my big solo. During those two seconds, I think, "Here it is . . . I'm going for it!" Then I plunge into an upward cascade of wildly spirited triplets, and the 9-foot roars ferociously, well above the full volume of the entire orchestra. The piano rages on alone, until a dramatic decrescendo is at last swallowed up by silence. Somewhere in the distance, the strings take over for good.

I hoped I could always recall that specific sort of joy.

Carol Rich

Periphery

I finally see it. I catch it watching me—it was hiding behind my busy mind. Its gaze shifts slightly as I become aware of it. It wonders what I'll do next—I can tell by how its toes lift slightly from the branch. It's a tiny Yellowthroat peeking out from a thicket. On another day, it's a skittish Virginia Rail that freezes mid-step when it sees me seeing it. Or, it's a hidden-in-plain-sight Great Horned Owl waiting for my obtuse human brain to "tune in" to its presence.

Whatever form it takes, when I stop to admire it, it gives me a look. I wouldn't call its expression one of surprise. It's more like it's thinking, "Oh bother. Now I have to watch *you.*"

Loste Derknes Fownde

The Cloud of Unknowing is a compilation of fragments presumed to have been written by a 14th-century monk. The subject matter: philosophy, theosophy, and spirituality. "Meeknes in itself is not ellis bot a trewe knowing and felyng of a mans self as he is."

To my untrained eye, the Middle English looked like anagrams. I realized that a fluid comprehension of this perplexingly familiar, foreign-language imposter required me to capture phrases by using a long visual sweep, which kept me from getting tripped up on quirky details. After gleaning the sentence's meaning, going back to decipher individual words was a snap. It was similar to training my hands to capture the harmonies and gestures of a seemingly unravel-able Scriabin Sonata. Proceeding at a normal pace worked better than stumbling over every note. My usual routine when I learn a new piece of music is to treat every marking in the score, "playing the ink," as we call it, with equal importance on the first read-through. With Scriabin Sonatas, detail work—fingerings, pacing, voicing, pedaling, mood and character—would come after. Having completed my first Scriabin Sonata, the 5th, which came midway between his Romantic period and a shift to a mystical, contemporary harmonic scheme, the later sonatas came with relative ease. By studying Scriabin, I'd developed a new skill, a fresh way to view the score. Developing the ability to read Middle English came to me in the same way.

"For when I sey derknes, I mene a lackyng of knowyng; as alle that thing that thou knowest not, or ells that thou hast forgetyn, it is derk to thee, for thou seest it not with thi goostly ighe. And for this skile it is not clepid a cloude of the eire, bot a cloude of unknowyng, that is bitwix thee and thi God."

This fragment, *On Darkness,* comforted the ill-illuminated corners of my soul where I suspected fear was lurking. I delighted in the visual beauty of the language. The spellings, which looked like fluttering leaves on a tree, were actually hundreds of butterflies about to take flight, which left the bones of the tree intact.

But more significant than the content, the physical book itself, *The Cloud of Unknowing,* was a beacon in dark times—and it came to me twice. The first was in 1976, when I was an undergraduate at Hartt.

I couldn't find the clerk anywhere. I waited by the register in the dusty, dimly lit Occult Arts bookstore. The book I was seeking, *The Cloud of Unknowing,* wasn't in the library or the big-name bookstores, but it *was* on the non-required reading list for my Music Theory VII class. We were required to read two books from the non-required reading list. Negotiating Theory VII was nothing if not puzzling. The book could be anywhere or nowhere. I went up and down the aisles and scanned the titles. The subject headings were of no help. I considered leaving. I waited. Wandering up and down the stacks again, I held onto a threadbare hope that my gaze would miraculously fall upon the enigmatic title.

I called to the back room. "Hello? Anyone there?" No answer.

Then, I noticed a purple-bound book sticking out from a sea of black bindings. I'd been down that aisle several times. Surely, I would've noticed a book that wasn't sitting flush with the others.

A beatnik lookalike came out from the back room.

"Find what you're looking for?"

"Not yet," I said. I went to the book and read the spine. "Never mind. I have it."

৯

When I graduated Hartt, I misplaced the book. I learned to live with the void that had formed in my soul where the book's wisdom used to be. It took me thirty-five years to seek it out again. I thought that surely, Powell's City of Books in Portland would carry *The Cloud*. Even locals need the store map to navigate Denali-sized Powell's. I scanned the map, but it was all too much. I had no clue where to start. I was stuck—again. I shuffled up to one of the many info counters. There were computers. There was Google. There were three clerks at that one info desk alone.

"Author's name?"

"Uh . . . don't know. He was a 14th-century monk."

"Title?"

"The Cloud of Unknowing."

About a hundred listings of *The Cloud* popped up on the screen.

"Editor or publisher?"

"Nope. Sorry."

"It's okay. Let's try this one."

I followed the clerk up two floors and deep into a deserted section of the stacks. We passed subject heading signs for Mysticism, Philosophy, Christianity, and Poetry, and finally came to a stop at the Christian Mysticism section. This clerk was good. He ran his hand along the titles where the book should've been.

"Hmm. Not here. That's odd. Computer says we have it in stock." He checked the shelves above and below. Even if we were in the right section and aisle, a misplaced book could stay hidden for a long time. "Nope. Not here. Sorry." His puppy-like eyes blinked. He shrugged.

I fully expected to see *The Cloud* sticking out from the other books. My senses tingled, and for a second I thought I could will it to appear. The stacks were about thirty feet long and six shelves high, plus an additional two shelves above for overstock. Then I spotted a narrow purple binding hiding between two huge, black, hardcover tomes on occultism in Christianity. It reminded me of a small, trembling, Ruby-crowned Kinglet flanked by two tall-shouldered, slit-eyed vultures.

"It's okay. It's up there," I said.

Puppy Eyes looped the step-up stool with his toe, dragged it to the spot, and hopped up to retrieve it. "I don't know how you saw that. Here you go."

It had the same cover and weight as I remembered. It also gave me the same sizzling sensation in my stomach—as if it was enchanted—as if it had decided to wait for me until I quieted myself and listened.

Carol Rich

Reflection of a Long-Haired Girl

When I was a kid, family vacations involved touristy destinations in New England, including impromptu stops at country stores, diners, and riverside motels. One summer, we spent a month at Conklin's Dairy Farm in New Hampshire. We milked cows, pitchforked hay in the barn, and did whatever chores needed to be done. The pleasantly personal aromatic interaction with the farm and its animals incited in me a love of—well—cows, hay, and barns.

One perfect-fishing-weather day, with just the right amount of cloud cover and not much wind, Bob and I were dropped off at the local pond, where we climbed into the lone rowboat and glided out to a spot by some lily pads, a place where fish would likely be hiding. Bob told me I was a natural oarswoman as he taught me how to change direction, drift to a spot without scaring the fish, and how to slow to a stop. I loved the sound of water lapping against the bow, and the *drip, drip, drip* of droplets falling from the oars after they were lifted with a satisfying *thud* onto the edges of the boat.

We cast our lines and settled back for a lazy morning on the secluded pond. Scanning the lily pads for frogs, I noticed several dark protrusions popping up out of the water. I realized with a delightful shock that they were the reptilious-periscope heads of turtles.

Bob cast his line again, and a sharp tug made my head jerk back. Bob's face drained of color.

Part Nine

"Hold still, sis. I mean it, don't move." He rummaged around in the fishing gear and shouted, "Damn it!" Then he clenched his fists and scrounged around in the bottom of the boat.

Something warm dripped down my face.

"Leave it. Here, this is the best I can do." He put a dirty rag over my eyebrows. "Hold this, but don't push on it. You okay?"

Bob's pale face turned bright red, and was streaked with gunk. He cut our lines, threw our rods into the boat, and grabbed the oars. We were back to shore in a few powerful strokes.

"Mom and Dad won't be back for hours. We'll have to walk. Leave your stuff in the boat. Come on." He grabbed my hand.

After a long, hot, dusty walk to town, we found the doctor's office that was really a single room at the back of his house. While he set up a tray of instruments, I tried to get a glimpse of myself in the mirror. Bob blocked my view. "Trust me, sis. You don't need to see that."

I'd been snagged right between the eyes with a three-hook lure. It just felt like something was stuck to my skin, like when you touch fly paper. The doctor cleaned the area and then wiggled the lure. I squirmed as I watched his old-man hands bring a syringe up to my eyeballs. "Lidocaine," he said. Blood oozed down my face when he cut the barbs and slid out the hooks. One more shot, tetanus this time. By the time I got a good look in the mirror, a rectangular bandage sat squarely in the center of my forehead, where my hair parted and fell in long ponytails to each side. I liked the symmetry.

Afterwards, back at the farm, I relaxed in the tree swing and looked out at the rolling valley. The screen door to the farmhouse banged shut, and Bob appeared carrying two frosty glasses of lemonade. He smiled feebly and handed me a glass. "Here you go, sis." He sat in an Adirondack chair next to the swing. Sipping our tart drinks, we watched Pet, the black and white family cow, saunter up the hill before plopping down between us to munch her cud.

Flight of the Red-Tailed Hawk

A year after Bob died, I visited the Quechee Gorge Bridge. I'd been there decades before, in the '60s, on one of our family vacations through Vermont and New Hampshire.

On that trip, I left my pink and white, hard-faced, stuffed animal named Bunny Doll, behind in a forested riverside motel on one of the many scenic byways. My little heart ached for the rest of the trip, which included a drive up Mount Washington, where, attempting to quell my sobs, Dad held me tight against the wind as we contemplated the sweeping view of the rolling mountains. Meanwhile, unbeknownst to me, Mom called the motel to have Bunny Doll shipped to our house where it would be waiting for me in a brown box closed with clear packing tape. It would spend all subsequent vacations safely on my bed at home. But despite the semi-detached face and plucked out stuffing of the near-fatal injuries later inflicted by Scrappy, it remained my second favorite "stuffed" animal.

Tim, my Teddy bear, who knew me better than anyone else on earth, retained all of his stuffing, which absorbed and safeguarded my childhood tears, despair, and fits of anger. He was stalwart, and he wore his scars like badges of honor: re-sewn seams, a reattached eye, plush-worn bald spots, and a permanent, circular neck divot that took the place of a discarded red ribbon. On subsequent summer vacations, Tim occupied a full third of my undersize, '60s-flower-power decorated plastic suitcase. At night, as a distraction from Dad's snoring, the inescapable odor of mold in the motels, and peculiar shadows that flickered on ornate wallpaper, I snuggled Tim close and sang quietly into his soft cheek until I fell asleep.

When Bob jumped from the bridge, he took many of my happiest childhood memories with him. I wanted to return to the spot, to Quechee Gorge, to feel it with my adult heart, to reclaim its beauty—even if it turned out to be a dark, gnarled sort of beauty.

My piano teacher's house in the Berkshires, just a couple of hours from the gorge, served as my home base: a zone of love and laughter from which I could sally out to the place of my brother's last breath. When I pulled away from her house, I was armed with courage and hope. I'd be back in a few hours—after.

As the Mohawk Valley dropped away in the rearview mirror, the rolling hills of Vermont and New Hampshire loomed ahead. I drove past village squares, country stores, and gazebos, but my heart was hollow. A sickening pain in my stomach threatened to freeze the towering trees and meandering rivers into a disturbing snapshot-memory. Pain oozed over everything, like hardening amber.

The town closest to the Quechee Gorge was White River Junction, where I finally forced my shaking foot to ease off the gas. I had to regain some sort of calm. Pulling onto the side of the road, I discovered that I was next to a country store, one that was guarded by life-size carvings of bear, moose, and elk. The towering heads of the wooden creatures were just as imposing as when I cowered below them in my childhood. The texture of timber-grooved fur, the bear's alarmingly glassy stare, claws and hooves buried in inches of hardened mud. Memories surfaced like festering splinters.

Stepping onto the wooden porch, I swung open the lightweight screen door and was suddenly surrounded by comfortingly mundane objects: Vermont T-shirts, mugs, homemade ice cream, fudge. I picked up a tin of Vermont maple syrup for Georgia and a small bag of Cape Cod chips for me. Getting back into the rental car, I braced myself for the next fifteen minutes.

I passed a historic sign for the Quechee Gorge. Then the road straightened out and I saw the bridge up ahead. The deck of the bridge looked like any other road lined with sidewalks and stone railings. Its unique architectural design and grandeur would be found in the structure beneath. The speed limit dropped to 15 mph, and I locked my gaze on a point beyond the bridge, where a sudden hillside signaled a sharp turn in the road. Cruising past the parking lot, I held my breath and spanned the gorge. Fortunately, there was a second parking lot on the far side, where I veered off the road and cut the engine.

When I opened the door, my glasses were instantly sprinkled with mist. Directly in front of my spot was a sign that gave the dimensions of the bridge: the length, the height of the supporting arched structure, and the flow of the rock-strewn river below. I knew all that I needed to know. It was high enough.

The earthy aromas of the evergreen forest made me homesick for the Pacific Northwest. Given that I grew up on the East Coast, the disorientation was alarming.

Releasing my grip on the car door, I dragged my body across the road. Gravity seemed to work against me as I stepped up onto the extra-high sidewalk that crossed the bridge. After a few paces, I was looking out into too-thin air—over the narrow gorge. There was less water and a lot more rocks and boulders down there than I'd expected. Panic rose in my chest. I'd have to do it quickly. I fished the Red-tailed Hawk feather out of my bag and let it ruffle in the breeze. I held it out over the edge. Then I let go.

Survival instinct got me back to the car, where I stared through the rain-streaked windshield at the rendering of the bridge, which I then noted was 165 feet above the Ottauquechee River. A sensation of the feather's texture lingered on my fingertips, and I had to look at my hand to make sure I'd actually released it. I couldn't breathe. My body shook. A film of condensation coated my glasses.

I thought about an article in the local paper that I'd found online, describing, in oddly detached language, my brother's actions that day.

Leaving the car door open, he ran from the far parking lot, raced past two tourists on the bridge, and vaulted the railing.

54

Five years had passed since I'd reached Bob's final age. He'd never be older than fifty-four.

One day, a little kid pointed at me and said, "Grandma!" Her mother looked to be about twenty. The comment that her daughter called everyone with gray hair "grandma" didn't take away the sting. When I got home, I looked in the mirror and saw the proverbial silver-haired woman looking back at me. She was older and a little heavier than I imagined, but when I looked deeper, her sparkling green eyes and reassuring grin tugged at my heart. I touched the small scar in the middle of my forehead. There are worse things than being Grandma to little kids.

My Soul as a Tree

Maybe after I die my soul will meld with a tree and that'll be that until the tree dies, or gets cut down, or the fungal connective tissue—the vital layer of biome beneath the forest floor—gets ripped away by bulldozers and my tree withers from loneliness. When the tree is gone, where will I go?

Part Ten

Northern Illusions

The forest was silhouetted against a cerulean sky. Effects of the extreme northern latitude lent the nighttime air a hypnotically celestial quality that made me see luminescent shapes in the trees, shapes that resembled wood nymphs, until I looked directly at them and they dissolved into the mist. A vibrant yellow caution sign by the trailhead stood out in relief against the two-dimensional, slate green landscape. There were bears and moose in the area.

We followed the Liard River Hot Springs trail to a boardwalk that meandered over an expansive maze of marshland, where willows' lithe limbs drooped over green-black water. The place was devoid of sound. There wasn't a single croak or passing buzz. Vibrations in the boardwalk made the algae and duckweed that blanketed the water move like gently undulating land.

Once, on a trip through the Tetons, we saw a moose in a marsh plunge its colossal head beneath the surface and come up with twigs sticking out of its mouth. Strings of mucky grass hung like tinsel from his impressive rack. I had to stifle a chuckle. But moose demand respect. It glared at us as water cascaded from its mouth. The moose's eyes and nostrils glistened as its jaws worked, cow-like, on its delectable marsh meal.

We'd seen that Teton moose in daylight. Now it was midnight in northern British Columbia. Creatures of the marshland would be swathed in gloaming's gray gauze.

A sign directed us to the final leg of the trail, where we slinked past a steep hillside of black boulders sweating with moisture. Rounding the corner, we were met by a wall of heat and the stink of sulfur. We'd emerged by a large hot springs that was blanketed in blue steam. Small lights edged the main pool as well as various offshoots that tumbled over rocks, walls, and stairs. When I eased into the hot water, my travel-bound muscles relaxed for the first time in weeks. We were swaddled in soft blue solitude. I thought about moose and bears as the long sweep of Bach's Double Violin Concerto played in my head. Wisps of water vapor wafted up into the forest, producing a subtle, steady, nearly inaudible hiss—like bows drawn across strings.

After our midnight soak, we retraced our steps through the woods, returned to the truck, patted the dogs on their sleepy heads, and drove away from the Liard River Hot Springs trail.

I have an abysmal sense of direction, but with the exception of two or three crucial junctures, our route so far seemed to follow one northbound road all the way through Washington, British Columbia, Yukon, and Alaska. As the terrain grew more remote, it *was* the only road. When it was my turn to drive, all I had to do was remember where we'd come from and point the truck in the other direction.

But, the ill-defined single-lane dirt/gravel road to the hot springs, which zigzagged through a field of boulders and scrub trees, provided ample opportunity to get turned around, especially in a twilight that demanded a sort of vision I simply didn't have. I left it to Georgia's superb directional sense to get us out.

After leaving the woods, we stopped in the field of boulders. The combination of the soak, twenty-two hours of daylight, and the cool night air left me euphoric. Neither one of us felt tired, but we wanted to cover a lot of miles the next day. Should we stay put and get some sleep right there in the boulder field? Or should we push on in hopes of finding a better spot?

Condensation from our hot-springs bodies quickly steamed up the windows, so naturally, we rolled them all the way down. There must've been something—a sound, a shift in light, a minuscule movement—that caught our attention. I didn't remember Georgia stopping so close to a boulder, but there was a huge one right next to her window. Then an eye opened in the middle of the dark shape. I couldn't figure out what it was, but part of my brain believed it was a boulder with a crazy big eye. It dawned on us simultaneously—bison! It was taller than the truck; its head would never fit through the window, but I didn't want to see it try. Bison are unpredictable and dangerous. It might decide it would be fun to ram the truck and roll it over.

I didn't understand why the aroma of wild bison didn't set off the dogs. They always barked at wildlife. They jumped up every time we so much as slowed the truck. At home, they even barked at the stone lions by the credit union.

One time, at The National Bison Refuge in Montana, we saw families of bison join to form a circle around their young. We learned that males, like the one that held our lives in its hooves, can be fiercely protective. They stomped at the ground, which sent up clouds of dirt between our car and their babies. One especially well-endowed male, who we dubbed "the uncle," sauntered in our direction, snorted, flashed its comically skinny tail, and pawed at the ground. We moved along before it had a chance to charge. That day, the herd was at least fifty yards away.

Suddenly, I worried that the bison belonging to the glaring eye in the window was part of a herd. Then I realized there were several bison scattered among the boulders. The slightest move from us could set off a stampede. Even rolling up the window would be foolish. We avoided eye contact, but it was challenging. The eye was so big! Viewing a bison from a distance gives the impression that the eye is proportionately small to its head, and that's true. It's a testament to how huge the head was.

Georgia started the engine and eased it into first. The bison didn't flinch. I held my breath as the truck edged ahead a few inches, then feet, then yards. In the end, the bison must've decided we weren't a threat. When I looked back, I couldn't single out ours from the dozens of bison standing still as boulders in the field of mist.

Mosquitoes

It started with an annoying buzz by my ear. Giving it a swat, I drew my blanket up over my head. I slumped down lower in the passenger seat and fell back to sleep. *Buzz, buzz.* It was under the blanket this time. I was disoriented and foggy-brained, but when I looked around, it was clear what was unfolding in the cocoon of our truck. Countless tiny black invaders were crawling in along the edges of the pass-through protector between the cab and the back. It was a full-on invasion. Frantically squishing as many as I could, I realized that closing the windows hadn't been good enough. The scent of warm blood lured hordes of fiercely determined mosquitoes directly toward our veins. Indifferent to the impermeable nature of glass and metal, they swarmed the truck like flies on a dead carcass.

I must've parked next to a marsh, something I would never have done had it been light enough to see. I kept killing the buggers, and soon the windshield was splotched with red and black. I heard Georgia slamming her hands against the windows, walls, and ceiling in the back. The truck rocked from our ineffectual killing spree. Everything, including me, was covered in blood and disembodied insects. The carnage was impressive, but the attackers were ruthless. If we didn't do something, we'd be mosquitoed to death.

"Get us the hell out of here!" Georgia shouted.

I grabbed my keys, climbed into the driver's seat, started the engine, and floored it.

"Open the windows!"

The mosquitoes were sucked out in a matter of seconds. Panting, I pulled over and looked through the pass-through. It was a miserable bloody mess back there. Georgia was wiping her hands on a dog towel. Our three dogs were panting and scrambling over each other. The truck's interior was a mortuary for mosquito parts.

After weeks on the dusty road, the truck was overdue for a good cleaning anyway, which we took care of at one of the carwash stations to be found in every town. I could've sworn that the locals smirked at us as we pulled in looking bleary eyed and bug ridden. We'd been hazed.

The Arctic Circle

The Alaska Highway was the geographical spine of our road trip. By the time we reached mile zero in Dawson Creek, B. C., I realized that merely getting *there* had been an accomplishment. After the prerequisite photos by the mile zero marker, we went to a Pioneer Town and Museum where, bizarrely, we were assaulted by the all-too-familiar, lingering odors of a centuries-old dentist office.

Driving along the Alaska Highway in the evenings, when we traveled with windows closed, K. D. Lang sang about *Western Stars* and *Big-boned Gals*. When it was my turn to drive, Bach Violin Sonatas and Brahms Symphonies propelled us through hundreds of wilderness miles. At milepost 1,314, in Tok, Yukon, a for-sale puppy sled dog we named Tok almost became the new dog in our pack. Fortunately, the decision to leave her there until our return trip south ended in someone else adopting her. We reached the terminus of the Alaska Highway at milepost 1,422 in Delta Junction, Alaska. Our other major destinations were Denali, Homer, and the Arctic Circle. Beyond that was a distant hope—Prudhoe Bay, a possible polar bear destination.

I'd wanted to see polar bears in the wild since I was a kid, but their habitat was fast deteriorating due to climate change. I'd dreamt of taking the train from New York to Montreal to Churchill, where I'd join a tundra buggy expedition and get close to polar bears. But I'd waited too long. Now the bears were struggling to adapt to a shrinking environment, and even though the tundra buggies continue to trek camera-laden tourists to the bears' hunting grounds, I have no desire to add to the stress.

Sadly, our goal to see polar bears in Prudhoe Bay was chancy at best. We'd already experienced the unanticipated and unpredictable driving conditions throughout British Columbia, Yukon, and Alaska, the most annoying of those being permafrost-heaved pavement and bowling-ball size potholes that appeared out of nowhere with only a circle of white warning paint around them that usually came into view too late to avoid a hazardous jolt. There were shifty mountain goats licking salt at the edges of the road, and continual repair on those permafrost-deformed roads. "Pilot fish" cars, our nickname for the lead vehicles, escorted long lines of RVs, campers, trucks, and cars through single-lane construction zones. Miraculously, the multitudes dispersed within minutes of passing the tanned, sweaty work crews.

By then, we were seasoned north-country drivers, but could we realistically make it safely to Prudhoe Bay? If we decided to proceed farther north, the phrase "poor road conditions" would take on a whole new meaning. Our Alaska bible, *The Milepost,* warned that a tow from anywhere on the road to Prudhoe Bay would cost at least $750. And turning around wasn't always logistically possible. It would be a commitment.

We stopped north of Fairbanks at the final truck-stop/restaurant before continuing to the Arctic Circle. It would most likely be our last contact with people for the next few hundred miles before terminating in Deadhorse on the North Slope near the Arctic Ocean and Prudhoe Bay. The very words made my heart race.

Parking on the packed dirt of a deserted, built-for-multiple-tractor-trailers parking lot, we fed and walked the dogs, grabbed our maps and travel guides, and went into the restaurant, the Hilltop. Two women traveling alone usually incited interest from the locals, and ogles were plentiful. Oddly, the service reminded me of a place near Juilliard and Lincoln Center called "Johns," where you were greeted through throngs of hungry diners by barking from the head waitress. "Coffee, honey? Sit wherever you want, I'll be right with you!" At the Hilltop, the waitress barked out orders in a language known only to the cook, and laughed good-naturedly when she pointed us in the direction of a table next to a hoary couple nursing their watery coffee and oversized homemade pastries. Then the food came out: eggs, toast, and two plates of greasy hash browns, each one the size and height of the waitress's beehive hair. Those mounds of potatoes gave us the courage to go on.

We learned that, even if we did make it all the way to Prudhoe Bay, a military post guarded the oil fields fifty miles south of the bay itself, and it wasn't guaranteed we'd be allowed passage. "Sometimes yes, sometimes no," one of the locals said. We decided that at the very least, we'd try for the Arctic Circle.

We filled the tank, applied sunscreen and Cutter, and headed north. The Dalton Highway, the quintessentially rough road we'd been on for over a hundred miles since its inception in Fairbanks, continued on as a haul road built for the construction of the Alaska Pipeline. It's known as one of the most challenging, isolated roads in the US and is featured in the show *Ice Road Truckers.* Drivers are advised to take survival gear. The minute our tires touched the dirt/gravel/mud/sand/permafrost road, life shook. We were on a dipping, sloping, steeply graded, washboard road that wended north for three hundred miles. The steering wheel vibrated, the dogs' collars jingled, my teeth rattled. We laughed at the absurdity of it, and quickly let go of the notion of making it to Deadhorse. We'd be shaken to death, "Like the horse the town was named after," I said.

Isolation. Tiny pink and white flowers dotted the tundra to the far reaches of the horizon. I anticipated seeing evergreen forests, but spindly shrubs were the tallest flora to grow from that harsh ground. The Alaska Pipeline, which sometimes skirted the road like a too-tall railing, or at other times ventured hundreds of feet away, was always in view except where it cut underground through steeply rising hillsides that would've added too much sudden altitude for the flow of oil. The pipeline itself, which sat in supports shaped like huge tuning forks, was retrofitted for earthquakes of 7.5 or less. But it was worrisome. Alaska was known for tremors of 9.0 and greater. I had no problem imagining an oil spill decimating the virgin ground that was gradually becoming less perma every year. I felt lucky that we had a chance to see the ice-blue glaciers in the north country while they were still relatively healthy.

The Dalton Highway, also known as The North Slope Haul Road, took us right up between where Kanuti National Wildlife Refuge meets Yukon Flats National Wildlife Refuge, both surprisingly devoid of wildlife. My guess was that our rattling, groaning truck announced our arrival a good ten miles away, allowing caribou, fox, and ptarmigans (parmesans, as we called them) to hunker down until we were past.

Success was measured in yards. The narrow, unpredictable "road" rarely allowed a place to pull over and de-stiffen our bodies, and when we did, our stops were brief. We wanted to touch the Alaska Pipeline, and eventually found a safe spot to pull over—one least likely to damage the permafrost. The pipeline dipped low enough in its supports for Georgia to touch her fingertips to the bottom of the forty-eight inch diameter gray pipe. I lacked the two extra inches it took to touch that particular section, but when I tried, my skin bristled. I was bear-anoid, and I sensed *ursus* energy coming from the other side of the pipeline. After posing for a quick pic, I sprinted the fifty feet to the car. Georgia laughed her ass off.

We rattled north once again. Our noisy isolation was only briefly interrupted by a couple of passing trucks that hauled unidentifiable, gargantuan metal objects toward Prudhoe Bay. We closed the windows as clouds of dust and debris billowed over us. We took great satisfaction as we listened to the *ping, zip* of rocks jumping off the headlight/radiator screen, which, taking strong encouragement from the Milepost to heart, Georgia had built for the trip.

Hours down the road, we spotted a dark object in the distance. It wasn't moving at all, so we ruled out a brown bear, caribou, or muskox. It turned out to be a large brown national park sign with a freshly painted depiction of The Arctic Circle in blue, green, and brown. The sign, with the designation of Latitude 66° 33', was beautiful, but so unexpected, so out of place—it was farcical. We pulled into the paved parking lot (!) and got out for a celebratory stretching of legs. Instantly, swarms of tiny mosquitoes were all over us, in our ears and mouths, and on the dogs' eyes and noses. We couldn't breathe or speak. We quickly kissed, eyes-and-mouth-closed style, and snapped a photo of the entire family by the Arctic Circle sign before diving back into the truck.

It took ten and a half hours to go three hundred and fifty miles, but eventually, we made it back. The tires were humming along on regular old, rough, potholed pavement again. Taking the next opportunity to unfold our limbs, we turned onto a deserted haul-truck-sized pullout. Our shiny red truck was now a lovely shade of mud-cake brown, and the dog faces that usually appeared at the back window were obscured behind a thick layer of tundra dirt.

To the near north, burnt orange swept across the sky's dome, where it softened to a gentle pink in the faraway south.

Denali

The 6 P.M.-11:30 P.M. Denali National Park excursion bus had a total of eleven people onboard. We hadn't planned on leaving the dogs alone in the truck for so long, but it was a cool night—they'd just sleep. Public car traffic is prohibited in Denali, and what roads do exist cover a tiny fraction of the six-million-acre park. The excursion was the best option.

The undercarriage of the full-size bus was built to handle the extreme curves we'd be navigating on our trip. The tires weren't on the ends of the bus, but in the middle. Some of the curves were sharper than ninety degrees, and the special configuration allowed the front end—driver included—and the rear of the bus, to swivel out away from solid ground into midair. Of course, for that to happen, the roads had to be railing-less. I wasn't a fan of this setup, but being in the park for the purpose of finding wildlife was worth the few seconds of fear it took to clear the curves. The bus and I took them one at a time. Georgia was giddy every time we slowed to five mph to glide around a curve. She'd look down over the edge and grin. I'd look down at my hands until the bus regained its composure.

The last time I was on a built-for-curves bus was in the Alps. I was seventeen and my high school concert band was touring Europe. I thought about our performances in Vienna, Verona, and Salzburg. I recalled my solo bows after playing Rhapsody in Blue at the Vienna

Opera House. I conjured the chimes that resounded in the plaza during our outdoor concert.

When the bus straightened out, I raised my eyes and saw snow-covered, 20,320-foot high Denali rising out of the vast terrain ahead of us. The mountain's proximity made my back press into the soft, school-bus-type seat.

It was high July, and the pre-midnight sun dusted the landscape with gold. Surveying the sprawling terrain that draped around the mountain, I spotted the antlers of caribou in the tall undergrowth by a meandering stream, but no brown bears. The driver's instructions were clear: we shouldn't say, "Look, over there!" or, "Wow, a bear!" No. We were to work together, to sit quietly and scan the landscape. If we spotted something, we were to say these exact words: "Stop the bus." The driver had to keep her eyes on the road, so it was up to us. Stopping in the middle of the dirt road felt so wrong, but we only saw one other vehicle during our five-and-a-half-hour excursion, and it passed us going the other way. It was the last outbound bus of the day, and as we later learned, its inhabitants got to see *our* brown bear emerge from a bush behind us after we passed.

The farthest reach of our excursion took us to Polychrome Pass, an extremely narrow, steep road with 500-foot drop-offs, which led to the only place we were allowed to step out, at a place called Polychrome Overlook. My mind reeled as it struggled to make sense of the distances, gently rising heights, and atrociously tall Denali. A golden eagle soared on thermals in the air *below* us. It was all so wonderfully unfathomable.

On our way back, Georgia pointed to a spot across the valley. "Stop the bus!" she said. The driver slowed to a stop. All heads swiveled to the right. All eyes scanned the expansive hillsides along the wide valley. There were three tiny, faraway dark dots high up on the hill. I raised my binoculars. Gray wolves!

But there was more. Four white dots were on the hillside about four inches ahead of the dark ones. That's how far away it looked when I held up thumb and forefinger. It's impossible to gauge distance in such a vast space. It could actually have been a mile or more between the two groups. The dark dots inched along the sloping valley in the direction of the white dots. Wolves were shadowing Dall sheep. When the flock moved, the pack moved. The driver said that sometimes they go back and forth across the sprawling valley hillside all day. She also said that one of the campsites had been closed due to wolves in the area.

The four Dall sheep on the hillside were cool, but we'd eventually have a closer view of wild sheep on a future trip through Colorado. They were long-horned sheep that time, and we were close enough to see the whites of their eyes. The macho males stomped and snorted and flew at each other while their thrashing hooves pummeled the head of their rival. They'd back away from each other, dazed and dusty, then they'd stomp and snort and charge again, this time with a full head of steam. Their lowered horns crashed squarely into the horns of their challenger. The choreography was vicious, the soundtrack—earsplitting. One by one, the weaker, or less willing, tip-toed away up the hill, letting the last two brutes fight it out. It was all part of the rut, the mating ritual. The smaller "ladies" huddled together a few miles down the gorge, no doubt mumbling amongst themselves as they listened in trepidation to the resounding *boom* of their potential mates.

It didn't matter that the wolves in Denali were so far away that they looked like fleas. Witnessing their existence in that undeniably vital place was resoundingly potent.

My brief time with Denali felt like I'd entered the pumping heart of nature itself. For the first time in my life, I understood a little bit about the mystical connection humans form with mountains.

Tiny Houses of Ninilchik

The turbulent whitecaps and surging tidal motion of Cook Inlet reminded me of portions of the Oregon Coast. But, out in the distance where the water would meet the sky, the snow-capped Aleutian Range rimmed the horizon to the far reaches, both north and south. My lungs greedily inhaled the crisp sea air. Inland road trips usually activate my yearnings for open water, but North had distracted me by satisfying lusts I didn't know I had—lusts for wilderness. There'd been countless marshes, lakes, and rivers, but the realization that I hadn't seen or heard tumultuous water didn't occur to me until we drove the Kenai Peninsula from Anchorage to Homer, where the landscape on our left changed from waterfall-garlanded cliffs to rolling hillocks of dazzling green grass, and the inlet water on our right was a constant, invigorating source of oceanic-like presence.

In need of gas, and hopeful that the handmade ice cream sign by the road wasn't lying, we left the Sterling Highway and followed a short dirt road down to the seaside village of Ninilchik, population 772. The dogs' noses twitched and reached into the salty air. Aside from one mosquito-infested swim in Watson Lake, Yukon, the site of our first net-hat donning, the dogs hadn't had the freedom of running or cavorting by water. When we opened the hatch, they leapt out of the truck and tore down to the beach as if flung from slingshots. Careening through the surf, they spun in the sand, and jumped for sticks and their neglected Frisbee until their muzzles were caked with sea salt and their coats were slick with Alaskan seawater.

The village itself was oddly disjointed. The lower section was nestled on three sides by the Ninilchik River, where slumping, dilapidated structures commiserated with a handful of well-preserved historic buildings from the late 1800s. Atop the bluff, the cleanly painted Eklutna Russian Orthodox church looked out over the water with an aloof but wizened eye. In 1964, the entire lower section, Old Ninilchik Village, had sunk three feet during the 9.3 magnitude Good Friday earthquake. As a result, the town's landing strip collapsed into the Cook Inlet. A utilitarian post-quake section of town, where ice cream and gas *were* to be found, sat nearer the highway, up on the bluff and farther down the Sterling Highway from the church and Old Ninilchik Village.

Historic signs informed us that in 1847, a handful of Russian settlers from Kodiak Island moved to Ninilchik and lived among the Aleut, Alutiiq, and Dena'ina native peoples. A village-centric Ninilchik-Russian dialect emerged. In 2009, when we pulled into town, individuals from the nine original extended Russian/Alaskan native families were the ones we saw smoking salmon and curing the flesh and skin of bear, caribou, and elk. They were also the ones pumping gas and dishing up generous scoops of homemade vanilla ice cream.

The thick mystique hanging over Old Ninilchik Village was intensified by aromas from the smokehouse and the stiffly blowing, briny air. A Russian cemetery sat on earthquake-heaved, weatherworn land between the sea and the bluff, where dozens of curiously tiny houses were scattered among headstones and large granite crosses. The houses were shorter than I, and were painted in bright colors of the Russian families buried in the basements. The splashy homage to lost ancestors stirred a sad longing in my Slavic blood, something uniquely, hauntingly—North.

North

Black spruce trees in their symbiotic relationship with towering quivering aspens; ubiquitous marshes where gigantic moose and caribou hid behind skinny stalks of cattails and grasses; hundreds of eagles perched in trees or standing on gravely banks of silty river deltas; permafrost dirt in the grooves of my boots; the all-night-long birdsong at Kluane Lake in Yukon; a baby moose standing on wobbly legs at the edge of the road, its blocky body masquerading as a rock outcropping until, at the last second, its head turns to look at us; Turnagain Arm, where bore tides leave vast mudflats in the bay; Portage Glacier; masses of floating blue ice; Homer's sea otters floating on their backs while prying open their mollusk lunches; the omnipresent scent of sage and pine; the chilly summer air; a black bear camouflaged as a big hole in the hillside; muskoxen wagging their weighty heads while grazing; the atmospheric light; the constant nearness of wild things; Denali rising dazzling white against a shocking blue sky. The purity of these things eased into my heart, and like the inexorably evolving movement of tectonic plates, my perception of my place in the world shifted. A fresh passion took over. I yearned to bring the essence of wonder into my teaching, my playing, and into everything I touched.

Part Eleven

Ashes

My portion of Bob's ashes came in a twist-tied plastic bag crammed into a small, square, nearly weightless shipping box. The black felt-tipped scrawl on top of the box belonged to my nephew Brandon, the eldest of Bob's three sons.

The box sat on the dining room table for at least half an hour before I opened it. For another half an hour, I stared into the open bag of my brother's cremains. He was just at my house. What was he doing in a plastic bag? I gripped the sides of the table and leaned in closer. Small chunks of bone and bits of red matter had survived the cremation. My fingertip grazed the light gray ashes. Smooth. Silky. A hard bubble rose in my throat and words spewed from my mouth like projectile vomit, "You idiot. Look what you've done!" I sobbed for an hour.

❧

"Mom, come quick!"

When I heard Bob's high-pitched cry, I threw down my Viewfinder slides, and raced into the hallway. Mom was already there, but when I tried to pass, her arm slammed into my chest.

It was dark in the boys' room, and my second effort to squeak past resulted in my shin colliding with the corner of the bunkbed. I could see Bob's silhouette. He was pointing out the window, up at the sky.

"Look . . . it's Santa!" Bob's upturned face shone with moon glow.

"I see it," said Mom. Her arm was around his skinny shoulders.

"Let me in!" I said.

"I can't believe he's really here," murmured Bob.

Dropping to the floor, I squeezed myself between the wall and Mom's legs, then I gripped the windowsill and pulled myself up. Two tiny red lights floated across the sky.

"See him, sis?"

My body shook with love for my brother. "He's two years older than me, and he believes that's Santa's sleigh," I thought. I felt a tight smile form on my lips. "Um hmm," I nodded. Bob weaved his fingers through mine.

Then the plane drifted out of sight.

The bag of ashes shifted in my hand. Wiping moisture from my face, I straightened my squished glasses and squinted at the plastic bag. Sleep was a crevasse, one I'd fallen into without warning.

Bob and I had drifted apart. Lies were told behind my back. I disengaged from my family, but no one seemed to notice. Then, after decades of silence, I got a call from Bob. He was depressed. He'd lost his job in the lab at Dartmouth. He was in denial about the permanence of his divorce. His heart was filled with regret. There was talk of infidelity and physical abuse. I asked what would make his life better. "Only one thing," he said. "If I could turn back time."

A year later, he came to Portland to visit me. We went to Multnomah Falls and Bonneville Dam on the Columbia. He stayed in the guestroom and I cooked breakfast for him. Georgia got to meet her brother-in-law. I thought it was a beginning, a reboot, a do-over. The ashes that were sitting on the dining room table told me otherwise.

The impersonal note he left in his apartment the day of his suicide read like a formula letter, as if it was written under the influence of emotion-numbing drugs. But the email I received two months before, was thick with unfiltered suffering.

I didn't get the job I wanted . . . [they] knew about my suicide attempts and depression (off of meds). I really wanted that job . . . the application did require disclosing police records . . . It's all very depressing.

Had a doctor appointment today. I'm 15-20 lbs overweight. Thinking about stopping eating for a while—a crash diet. I know that this is not a healthy approach but I don't even care. I rarely feel hunger anyway—think it's the stress and depression.

Maybe I just have really bad Karma from killing so many thousands of mice [in the lab at Dartmouth] over 25 years.

At the rate I'm going I only have about one years living expenses left. This makes me feel sick to think about. I kind of feel like I've been living in hell for the last 3 years. It was great to visit Ken and you on the west coast. I do get some joy out of life. But, to tell the truth, I kind of wish my life would just end. There's almost no joy to be found for me. But we can't go back in time and change our mistakes. And, we can't trade lives with someone else.

My portion of Bob's cremains lives behind the small glass door on the upper shelf of the antique music cabinet I inherited from Birdie. I visit the ashes like people visit a gravesite. Lifting the hefty moose-decorated lid from its small porcelain bowl, I reminisce with Bob's bone chunks. They're a miracle—a part of him that will never go away.

Carol Rich

Jump the Water

I placed a hundred and twenty-five dollars cash on the clerk's desk: the cost of five nights' stay at Ecola Lodge in Cannon Beach, Oregon. The dewy, downy grounds included a badminton net, two Adirondack chairs, and a wooden swing hung from the limb of an old gnarled oak. Across a narrow inlet, the view from my rickety, wooden balcony revealed the line where, about an eighth of a mile away, an overcast sky met the steel gray water of the Pacific. A large herd of Roosevelt Elk gathered to graze in a small field across the dirt/gravel road where black, white, and brown bunnies twitched and hopped in the green, green grass.

It was the first full week in August of 1989, and Sunday morning brought a dozen or so people into town for coffee or breakfast before strolling down the beach under the cooling marine layer of clouds, which, I later learned, would reliably burn off by noon. Mist settled on my hair. A happy creature cooed in my chest.

The next day, on my way to work, I waved to the boarders who were playing cards by their first-floor picture window. They nodded a squinty-eyed, *good morning,* while ash, the length of a fake fingernail, clung to cigarettes which dangled from their lip-sticked mouths.

By the time I reached the road, my Reebok high-tops were coated with dew and slippery grass bits. Pausing on a bridge over the inlet stream, I scanned for signs of non-human wildlife. There were wide trails, possibly muskrat or beaver, in the mud that circled around under the bridge and up into the reeds. Swallows soared over the water, and higher up, terns squawked and wobble-hovered as their wings and legs splayed out beneath their svelte bodies. A Common Merganser family rode the stream's gentle current, and below the water, their orange feet propelled them forward as if they were riding submerged paddle boats. Every few seconds, one of the mottled babies spastically darted out of line before regaining its spot among its fussing siblings. A Great Blue Heron floated down from its nighttime perch in the evergreens to trawl the tide-driven stream. Standing knobby-kneed in the shallows, it tilted its head in concentration and waited for glittering movement in the water.

I'd once seen a great blue snag a turtle and swallow it whole. The turtle-shaped bulge in the heron's neck made my own throat constrict. It was the first time I'd witnessed this shocking culinary habit of avian life. Since then, I've seen a vole-shaped bulge painstakingly wriggle down the lengthy, temporarily disfigured throat of a Great Egret, and I once watched in horror as a diamond-shaped sunfish stretched the insides of a Pied-billed Grebe's stubby gullet.

Every day at 4:15, on my way back to the lodge, I scanned the inland side of the bridge where horses grazed beside the stream in a boggy, bunny-happy field. Standing like ill-placed messengers of doom, cormorants, whose heads flopped freakishly to one side, rested on field boulders and exposed their full wingspans to the afternoon sun. Fidgety flocks of sopranos—starlings—roosted like shiny, noisy ornaments in the scraggly trees.

The Haystack Festival, the choral conducting workshop for which I was hired to play in exchange for the cost of my lodgings, convened in a hangar-like elementary school gym just across the inlet. Eight singers from Choral Cross-ties, the chamber choir I played for, led by the highly esteemed and beloved Bruce Browne, were hired as "ringers" for the workshop choir. Their strategic placement provided a core sound that filtered through every individual in the group, including me. The ringers led by example, and tirelessly—joyfully—put forth the highest musical, ethical, and professional standards. All members of the workshop choir—seasoned musicians, students, and novices—were equal participants in the eyes of the unwritten manifesto of the festival. A magical brew of compassion and humor from the master teacher, Rod Eichenberger, and the choir's phenomenal standards, made the five days of sight-reading through some 200-odd pieces followed by an under-rehearsed, yet polished, Friday night concert, an exhilarating joy.

After two summers at the Ecola Lodge, where the cursory nod from the boarders had become part of my daily routine, I was moved to a two-room beach house equipped with a single twin bed. The no-frills, hobbit-like digs put me within steps of both the school gym and the beach. That year, I began to notice the unusual number of gays and lesbians in the choir. The subterranean feed of energy from their knowing glances excited the creature in my chest. My first-week-in-August-at-the-beach job was peopled by kindred spirits.

The following year, I was the only occupant in an eleven-bed cottage, which sat half a block from the beach. Mornings, after a brief nod to the ocean, I got to work early and sought out my "lavender" friends, some of whom weren't "lavender" at all. But that was irrelevant. The gravitational pull between us was undeniable.

It wasn't a conscious decision that I'd spent most of my life among musicians. It simply happened. But for whatever reason—the nearness to the sea, the juxtaposition of music and nature, the integration of solitude and community, the soulful sincerity of human voices—I had to acknowledge the narrow description I'd attached to myself. I was in my mid-30s, and I realized with a start that I was having my inaugural experience with a family of gays and lesbians. We were musicians, but that was merely the medium through which love passed.

My lodgings changed yearly, but none lured me under its spell more than the it's-got-to-be-haunted, but in a good way, Gray Whale Inn, in nearby Tolovana. There were two floors of cozy rooms, but the week I stayed there, I was the sole—and last ever—occupant. At dawn, I watched through my window as the octogenarian proprietors lugged buckets of seafood guts to the gulls on the beach. At dusk, the husband and I played four-hand music on his resonant Steinway upright. As I lay on my bed at night, ocean breezes wafted thoughts of *staying forever* through the billowing curtains. I dozed and savored my dreamlike memory of a past not even an hour old.

Above the watery horizon, thin lines of charcoal clouds cut through the coral sun like embroidered felt. Lifting the collar of my sweater, I got in the car and pulled away from the Gray Whale Inn. Coastline-clinging 101 wended through an evergreen-shadowed, ocean-vista-peeking wormhole of a corridor. Emerging from a set of corkscrew turns, I was met with a startlingly close view of Haystack Rock, which sat unflinchingly in the flowing skirts of the silky, gray Pacific.

The "lavender" party house was festooned with pink and violet balloons, crepe paper, and rainbow flags. When I pushed past the streamers, which hung across the front door, a cheer of "Carol!" rolled through the room. My friends' eyes glimmered with kindness. Their expressions revealed fuller versions of their reserved, secret-identity workshop personas. Suddenly, I was being fed, hugged, and adored.

Bunched together by the picture windows, we admired the sunset-horizon beyond the 235-foot monolith, where long lines of silhouetted pelicans wafted down low over the water to reemerge seconds later from below the curling surf. On the rock itself, extended families of gulls were involved in a complicated version of musical chairs; the flapping squawkers obsessively repositioned themselves to make room for each other and the occasional puffin visitor. When the sharp edge of the sun dropped below the ocean's curvature, long fingers of azure and lime green flared up across the sky. We toasted to the future, to love, to freedom, to the savory spread before us, and to old and new friends—our chosen family.

The following year, Georgia and I stayed in a beach house on the inlet, which we, and two generations of pups, came to think of as our second home. Three doors down from the teensy hobbit house, the beach house had extra rooms, a real kitchen, fireplace, outdoor fire pit, and a front porch, where we perennially hung a windsock, signaling our presence to our friends. Steller's Jays, Downy Woodpeckers, and Rufous Hummingbirds were regulars. I learned the difference between the morning and evening songs of the gregarious White-crowned Sparrows.

For many years, the rental wasn't consistent, and I stayed, for good or bad, wherever I was placed. One summer, the aromas which constantly wafted up into my newly modernized apartment-rental over the downtown pizza joint, challenged my restraint daily, activating a resurgence of aroma-memories of the 24-hour chicken place ten stories below my apartment in New York.

Another year, I stayed in a dimly lit house on an ocean-side cliff, where a bramble-blocked, edge-clinging, railing-less path led to the front door. One night, having fallen asleep with a book on my face, I dreamed that twisted vines and roots penetrated the walls and threaded through my hair and around my throat. My family's return to the house on the inlet became a deal-breaker.

By 2016, cars, too large for Cannon Beach's parking spots, blocked the intersections. The traffic, which descended the road from the 101 into Cannon Beach, reminded me of the Long Island Expressway, known as, "the longest parking lot in the world." The parking spot in front of our beach house was often illegally blocked by tall, over-packed vehicles. Tourists, faces puffy and ripe with betrayal of the frigid Pacific, shivered in their bathing suits and flip-flops as they sauntered down the bustling sidewalks.

The line at once-intimate Insomnia Coffee reached out to the sidewalk. Struggling with the steady clamor that churned like crinkling paper around my ears, I scrambled for precious quiet time. The patrons played videos on their phones—at full volume. Cliques of kids from the Christian retreat center, which had taken over the north end of town and seemed to creep, Steven-King-style, toward the south end, cavorted and cackled like hyenas. Remains of their prey were left behind on the tables: crumbs, coffee cup rings, half-finished specialty drinks, gum wrappers, and lipstick-stained napkins.

I decided that my twenty-seventh year as pianist for the workshop would be my last.

❧

Standing alone on the sand, I recalled my first breath of crisp, wild, Pacific Ocean air, which I first tasted from the balcony of the Ecola Lodge. The ocean air proved to be a loyal friend—someone who told the truth, no matter how hard it was to bear; whose phantom body walked beside me on the beach and brushed the hair off my face; who, without my having to say a word, knew what was in my deepest heart. She whispered secrets that wafted into my dreams. She consoled my loneliness by showing me her long view of life. Whatever her mood—mist, driving rain, or warming sunshine—she was always there for me.

Yet, I knew about the coastal wind's dangerous winter relationship with the waters of the Pacific. Upon my return every August, I'd discover evidence of their tumultuous affair. Disheveled blankets of shoreline habitat had displaced mammoth amounts of sand leaving behind new acreage of dunes and temporary deltas. One year, my favorite lunch spot—a perfectly shaped indent in a weather-tossed, old-growth tree trunk—had been heaved down the beach, and a new, deeper mouth of the inlet carved a fresh passageway inland.

But every year, at the northern reach of the beach, no matter what catastrophic changes had happened through the winter, I'd reliably find the next generation's skittish Killdeer scooting from mound to mound in order to lead predators—me—away from its nest. It was playing a shell game. "You'll never find the right grassy mound!" she screeched. I always pretended she was right.

❧

At the end of day, my toes welcomed cool sand into their shyly exposed human inlets. Mist moistened my hair and glasses. The creature in my chest cozied down in a corner of my heart.

I'd seen the elk herd only one other time since that first morning in 1989, but their presence lingered, especially at dawn and dusk. I thought of my dear childhood dog, Scrappy, who, after once finding a small frog by the front door, checked that spot every subsequent day of her life. Hope was ongoing.

As I began my last grand stroll to Haystack Rock, salt air evoked a flood of memories: friends' radiant smiles, moon glow on waves' crests, spooky acoustics at freakishly way-out low tide, huge salmon bumping against the deep sides of the inlet as they surged toward their spawning ground upstream, the circle of friends standing hand-in-hand—quietly revering the mauve sunset after scattering the ashes of a beloved friend and lover.

But on that last day, halfway to the rock, approximately two hundred and fifty corgis were cavorting on the beach in anticipation of the annual Cannon Beach Corgi Parade. Feeling like a ghost of my own past, I held my memories close to my heart while I maneuvered unhindered through the darting, yapping throngs of short-legged pups.

Between the corgis and the Rock, dozens of gulls faced into the wind and hunkered down on the sand. They sidestepped, shifty-eyed, as I strolled past. The Rock itself was devoid of avian wildlife, but at its feet, tide pools displayed orange and purple stars clinging to life, seafoam green sea urchins undulating with the tide, and crusty black mussels grouped in tight conglomerations on shiny black rock.

The sea urchins made my heart lurch. I recalled a family vacation to California: a gag-inducing stench, a sideways smile on Bob's face as he held up a plastic bag containing a slimy, sand-infested sea urchin, the *thud* of the bag as it hit the bottom of a garbage can at a gas station, driving all week with the red rental convertible's top down in hopes of clearing out the stink. "He was a biologist in the making," I said to the sea.

At sundown, I took my camera to the north end of the beach to get an ocean's vantage point photo of modernized Ecola Lodge. In spite of the omnipresent murmur of tourists milling about by out-of-sight, faraway Haystack Rock, my part of the beach was deserted. I clicked off some shots of the lodge, which peeked through a break in the trees. When the sun lowered to offer its orange hue, a Common Merganser pair took center frame in my lens. A Killdeer zipped through the air, screeched, and landed in a tuft of dune grass ten feet from where I stood. "Shell game?" it offered. "Not tonight," I said. A Great Blue Heron stealthily emerged from a tall patch of grass by the shore and wafted up—*whoosh, whoosh*—to its evening perch in the upper boughs of an evergreen.

Standing on the sand, I reviewed my shots. At the bottom of the frame, in the same field where I saw the elk twenty-seven years ago, a large female elk was grazing. When I looked up, there she was, being joined by two smaller females. Then, out of the undergrowth, eight more Roosevelt Elk emerged. A Haystack family: a full-racked male, a single pronged male, the head female with dark brown, mane-like fur hugging her long neck like a custom-made muff, six adolescent elk, and two youngsters.

Seconds later, from out of nowhere, two human kids ran down to the water's edge and squawked at the herd. I could just see the elk rolling their eyes, but they kept grazing. Then, two cackling teenage girls in kayaks came splashing down the stream. Water sprayed around them as they pummeled each other with their oars. The elk froze. Their ears flattened against their heads. Calling out my pleas for respect only made the splashers cackle louder. The herd quickly fell into formation behind the head male and female, and while the single-pronged male took up the rear, three elk in the center formed a triangle with their heads—each one looking out in different directions. Three others looked to the rear, toward the kayakers. All of a sudden, the herd took off. It was a full-on stampede! Their hooves pounded the turf. The ground shook. Holding my breath, I tried to quell the tremors that traveled through my arms into the camera.

The buck led the charge through a field of tall grass, and suddenly, he was airborne. Pushing my shaking camera into my cheek, I captured the moment of his majestic leap over the widest part of the rivulet. The head female was next. She left the ground without the slightest hesitation, and landed without breaking stride. Single file, the rest of the herd followed: some landing belly-flop style on the far bank, some seemingly flying across like wingless Pegasus, and some stopping short—losing their running start—before cautiously launching over the water. But, one of the youngsters was left alone on the other side. Her mouth hung open in panic as she backed away from the rivulet and stopped about twenty feet away. The herd waited as she gathered the courage to execute, what must've been, her maiden voyage into the air. After what seemed like a full minute, she bounded through the grass and leapt, pixie-like, over the rivulet, where she alit on the other side, into the protective, fully formed circle of the herd.

With nostrils flaring and antlers raised high, the head male surveyed the area while the rest gathered so close together, their sides touched. After one last sudden, tight-knit charge toward the woods, the herd stopped to look behind them one last time.

Part Twelve

Carol Rich

Old Bones

No one noticed when I lifted my hands over the keyboard. But when I played the opening phrase of the Aria from the Goldberg Variations, the taciturn faces of the residents gawked, wide-eyed, in my direction. They were spooked rabbits, and instead of being caught mid-sprint, they were caught mid-catatonia. A woman in a red, boiled wool jacket raised her sunken-cheeked face and smiled. Lifting her shaking arm, she pointed at me and blurted out, "Look! It's a miracle!"

I knew that once Mom spotted me, music would be prohibited. I'd spent three nights on a train followed by a long drive in a rental car, yet, when I finally arrived at the independent living facility on Cape Cod, my first destination was the shiny, out-of-tune piano in the lobby. After the Bach, I played a Chopin Nocturne and a Medtner Fairy Tale. Then I wheeled my bag down the hallway to Mom's door.

A flick of the wrist—bits of Mom's breakfast landed in three close-knit spots on the plate: a tooth-marked scrap of English muffin, a morsel of unformed, slightly wet egg, and a masticated piece of muffin with a thin filament of cheese falling to the plate like the innards of a vole dangling from a branch. The toss-offs weren't given a sideways glance. The stringy, clotted, cheesy guts made my throat constrict.

Conversation was a jumble of yarn. If any two pieces accidentally or intentionally touched to form a semblance of beauty or structure, it was perfunctorily terminated.

I asked about her radiation treatments. Her eyes glazed over. Her stiff, gnarled fingers hadn't moved since the flick.

"Your treatments, Mom?"

"Don't you know how to play something other than that heavy Classical stuff?"

And there it was. The bone of contention. Apparently, news of my impromptu performance had traveled down the gossip highway, and I couldn't go anywhere in the building without being asked to play. My mother frowned and shook her head. I'd gone behind her back and played for the residents. I was supposed to feel ashamed. I did.

Her deformed fingers scraped at her napkin. Resistance boiled up from my stomach.

"I mean, don't you have everything memorized by now?"

"Yes Mom. I know all the music."

I wilt.

Carol Rich

Delirium

Mom was in the hospital. Blood loss, disorientation, dehydration, prescribed opiates, advanced age. The perfect storm for delirium.

For the first time in her life, she shared her thoughts with me, albeit over the phone after I returned to Portland. Mom had never suffered from dementia, so it was oddly fascinating that what she shared were delusions: glowing red-eyed gorilla gangs led by Ken chasing her down the hospital halls, and an eyelid-less doll—which turned out to be the nurse-call device—glowering at her while she tried to sleep. There were also sweeter, flitting-bluebird hallucinations about dining at a fancy boathouse restaurant with her pastor, which in reality was her sitting alone by the window while she ate boiled chicken and carrots from a hospital tray. She strolled along hedge-lined paths in an arboretum, which was actually an overnight, hours-long, walker-assisted shuffle around the nurses' station.

Because of her uneven pupils, there was talk of a stroke, which a CT quickly disproved. But an unnamed cancer was confirmed, and even though one of the doctors finally figured out how to stop the vigorous flow of blood from her vagina, bleeding out at some point was still highly likely. She was given two to ten months to live. Even so, two weeks later, after swiping at her nurse and screaming, "I'd rather die than take those drugs," she was stabilized and back home in the independent living facility where friends and staff called her "a sweet lady."

I knew I had to make another trip across the country to be with my mother. Time was short, and I was determined to make gentle, loving contact with the woman who had never crossed the line into "sharing one's feelings." Maybe now she'd accept love from her only daughter. It was my last chance.

She was uncharacteristically attentive when I reminisced about high school friends I was still in contact with, including a guy named David, whom I briefly dated. But as I suspected, Mom's quiet focus was a smokescreen for insidious goings-on in her brain—the placement of landmines for me to trip over at an unexpected point in my future.

That afternoon, at lunch in the dining hall with her friends, Mom said, "I used to date a boy named David." Her wildly mischievous eyes were at odds with her innocent expression. While I deliberated whether to feign interest in her blatant lie or to gently defy a true delusion—the choices suggested to me by her care nurse—her gaze steadied. "I know he was quite a bit younger than me," she said. I sighed and watched sweat bead up around the edges of my chocolate mousse.

The next day, I shared my Ancestry DNA test results with her: 49% Ukrainian, 50% Austrian, and 1% Finnish. Her response was that we needed to go down to dinner. It was already 4:20 and someone would steal our table if we didn't get there first. Her remark at dinner with her friends: "I had my Ancestry done and they tested my DNA. I'm Ukrainian, Austrian, and 1% Finnish." "Isn't that interesting!" said her friends.

Marveling at the blatant sass on my mother's face, I regarded the uneven pupils of her unwavering gaze. A swirl of steam formed in my chest.

The innocuous eye condition is called anisocoria, which was most likely sustained from falling face-first down a long flight of cement stairs decades ago. The disparate black pupil-holes disturbingly fortified her indecipherable facial expressions. Her fall is one my clearest memories, not because of the grapefruit-size lump over her eye, or the sound of the plastic garment bag getting caught in her feet. What crystalized the event in my mind was her comment as they carried her to the ambulance. "Why aren't you wearing a hat, Carol? It's snowing out."

I looked around the table at Mom's friends and sighed. One of them smiled at me.

All I could do was trust that some sliver of my love would find its way into my mother's heart.

Trees

"They're only trees!" In the intimate acoustic of the sleeper car, my voice sounded close and small. The snow-dusted landscape sparkled with iridescence. "So beautiful." My chest heaved with unexpected joy. Pushing my cheek against the window, I searched for the tops of the quivering aspens. Beyond the thin veil of branches, way out in the distance, massive pink- and blue-tinged glaciers blanketed the sweeping mountainsides and valleys. Large wings in my chest unfolded, and with one mellifluous flap, sweet, sweet air rushed into my lungs.

In a freak act of synchronicity, I saw my twentieth lifetime moose hiding its humongous frame behind the same stand of slender trees I'd admired during my eastbound journey.

The body has its own memory and mine is usually stronger than my will. I recalled a different train trip through Glacier National Park—also en route to see my mother. *It* occurred in darkness. Beyond the dizzying reflection of the window, forests, rocky mountainsides, and expanses of glaciers sat under the moonless sky. I tried to visualize them. But the swirling, undulating fluid in my brain had triggered paralyzing panic. The train's long strand of blue lights curled around a turn before being snuffed out. We'd entered a tunnel. The sudden change in air pressure made my eardrums feel like they were being squeezed by my long-ago-conquered lurker. The stiff curtain by my shoulder hung at a freakish slant. We were ascending. I gripped the armrest and fought against the swirling sensations in my head. Blinking hard, I tried to focus on the blue nightlight by my feet. As the train slid precariously around the sides of visually unverifiable mountains, I was swallowed up by the disorienting darkness of my father's workshop. A knee pushed into my chest. I was suffocating.

Shaking off the body-memory, I loosened my grip on the armrest and forced out the words, "I'll be okay from now on." I gazed at the shining, three-dimensional world beyond the glass. The snowy mountainsides' magnitude of distance and size made my chest swell with joy again. "It's so beautiful," I uttered. The sound of my breathing was a companion that had been in hiding in my breast pocket for decades. Freed at last!

I felt the presence of trees all around me—for miles and miles they surrounded me with lovely, sweet, dignified existence. I was among friends. It was all nature and me.

I'd been wondering why I hadn't cried during the visit with my ailing mother. But saying the words, "Trees, I love you. You're so beautiful," released tears from my eyes until I sobbed with joy.

I'd left home prepared to help Mom die. But my stubborn, mean-willed mother rallied. While we shared our last meal, her gaze was on the kids and grandkids surrounding her friend at the next table. "Now *there's* the kind of family I should've had," she said. Then she told me she didn't want me to play at her funeral.

When it came time to leave, I put my lips on her soft cheek for what I knew would be the last time. "I love you, Mom," I said. "If you say so," she replied. I physically felt the walls of my heart harden until I felt nothing at all.

As end-of-day light filtered into my sleeper car, I sobbed and scribbled these words on a scrap of paper: "Be brave. Enjoy your life."

Carol Rich

Surprise Ending

Nonresponsive. It was the best possible word.

When I turned onto my side, mud slogged around in my gut. Xen repositioned herself in the hollow of my stomach. Zoe's eyes twinkled as she looked up at me from the crook of my elbow.

"There will be no extraordinary measures for Hania," said the doctor. "The infection is very serious, and she's ninety-three."

Staring into the bleak predawn light, I buried my fingers in the soft fur behind Zoe's ear. Moisture fell sideways down my face.

We kids were forced to make up for ruining Mom's life by scrubbing away scuffmarks we'd made in the hallway. Nothing ever fully got the scars out.

"Her heart and chest are still warm."

"They probably wrapped her in warming blankets, Ken."

"Do you want a lock of her hair?"

"No. Just ashes. Thanks."

A few hours after Mom took her last breath, I lifted my face to meet a sundrenched mist that fell from a steel gray sky. It was a phenomenon—a blatant message from Mom, or God, or my own soul. My arms opened to let it into my heart.

❧

Sinking into the couch, I turned on *Grey's Anatomy,* where a resident's mother was dying of breast cancer. "Change the channel," I said to myself. "This is like the bridge-jumper show. Oh . . . it'll be fine. This is a mild version of mom death. Plus, mine didn't die of breast cancer, or any kind of cancer. I can take it."

I sipped my mint tea and let Zoe and Xen bookend me in place. My head relaxed against a cushion. Despite a glaring realization of being detached from my emotions, I prepared to let sleep take me, if it wanted to.

I'd taken Georgia to the airport at 4 A.M. that morning. Despite her offer to stay with me—that she couldn't stand the thought of my grieving alone again—her dive trip to the Philippines had been anticipated for so long. I convinced her to go.

At the next commercial, I lifted two sleepy dog heads off my lap and went to zap the rest of my tea. Suddenly, what had been a peripheral awareness of energy rushed past me like a charging grizzly. The house was dark, and the corner of the music room where Bob had made an appearance the night he killed himself six years ago was pulsating. I didn't want to acknowledge the energy field. That was Bob's corner. I flipped on all the lights. I said nothing.

Collapsing in on herself, the *Grey's Anatomy* resident shut the eyelids of her deceased mother. I envied the immediacy of her grief. Then, the TV screen went to black and the over-voicing said, "Goodbye, Mom."

"Are you kidding me?" I shouted.

❧

Dad's fingers were intertwined with Mom's. They were walking around the cranberry bog behind their house. Hoods hid the backs of their heads. Dad pointed to something on the pond. I woke up before they rounded the far end of the path. I never got to see their expressions.

It was the first time I'd hesitated before lifting my hands over the first notes of the Goldbergs. Mom requested that her pastor's teenage daughter play at her funeral. As I dropped my hands into the opening phrase, a sob collapsed my chest. Mom's service was over three thousand miles away. If her ghost had made the trip to be near me, she'd have to deal with how I mourned.

Mom's ashes arrived in a miniature box—two square inches of inanimate leftovers. Dozens of photos accompanied the package sent by Ken, including nesting Ukrainian dolls, a framed photo of Dad as a boy, and a photo of my twenty-something, pre-kids, pre-war mother engulfed in the arms of the man who was meant to be the love of her life.

Part Thirteen

Truth

It was just an odd pattern of color and light. Backing away, I clicked off some shots. I had no idea what it was or if it was anything at all. Inching closer, I took advantage of the momentary break in cloud cover to get a more vivid round of shots. At first, all I could decipher of it were the reds and browns of the leaves through what appeared to be a thin, black vein pattern of some sort. It was only after my brain registered the veins and wings for what they were, that the head, thorax, and blue-black-rust-yellow mosaic tail came into focus. Over the mottled colors of the fading autumn leaves, a dragonfly rested, hanging straight down, with its transparent, orange-edged wings fully extended.

It would take me a decade to learn that it was a female Blue-eyed Darner, *Rhionaeschna* multicolor.

Tiny Lives

I felt my vision deepen. My gaze landed on a swirling bumblebee. Its heavy body was covered in orange fur.

I tell my students, "There's a difference between hearing and listening. Sure, when we play, we hear sound coming from the piano. But listening is a skill. A conscious decision. It requires honesty and practice."

I'd spent my life fine-tuning my listening skills while simultaneously contemplating the superstructure of a piece. Observing macro-details in nature was a natural shift in focus. But it still required practice, plus a purposeful, respectful awareness of surrounding habitat—the superstructure.

I discovered pollen-slathered honeybees, as well as the pollen pouches hanging like goiters from their coal-black legs. I delighted in the bendy antennae of a cabbage butterfly, the geometrically patterned metallic blue and green back of a bottle fly, the shiny-smooth shell/wings of a yellow two-spotted ladybug, and the long filament-thin tongue of a butterfly moth. There were tiny, swollen, one-spotted, pink-eyed, white spiders too. Praying mantises had triangular heads and dragonfly-like eyes held at curious angles atop long stick-figure bodies. I chuckled at their tightly fitting, green snorkeling "shorties" that ended at elbows and knees. A diamond-shaped, lime-green aphid provided stunning contrast with the vibrant hue of a purple tulip.

One morning, there was a weird looking bee buzzing around in a sun-filled yellow bloom on the Missouri evening primrose in our front yard. Except for its royal blue eyes, the bee's body was emerald green with accents of black legs, antennae, and wings. Its black and white striped thorax was covered in fuzz. Specks of orange pollen clung like leg warmers to the green bee's knees that wrapped around one of the flower's delicate filaments. The bee tilted its head to one side and looked directly into my eyes. The bitsy orange pompom atop the flower's filament bounced up and down.

My new obsession clung to the underside of a leaf, touched tongue to nectar, and crawled along the edge of a blade of grass. I'd unearthed a profound love for the shape, color, and especially the personality of insects.

The skimmer's skinny little feet made depressions in the water's surface, like four bitty spoons resting atop the skin of chocolate pudding. When it moved, it didn't accelerate or slow down. It was simply in one spot, and then, *zip,* it was in another.

Farther out from the dock, blue damselflies did tippy-toed handstands on green pond slime. Others were freakishly hooked together in flight or resting in tandem on floating twigs.

Reaching for my binoculars, I found two dragonflies hooked together in the upper branches of an elm tree. Like the damsels, the tip of one's tail was attached to the top of the other's head—engine to caboose. Dangling from a leaf, the Olive Clubtail pair was exquisitely camouflaged among green and brown veiny leaves.

Dozens of dragonflies flashed their bold colors in the pond's dappled light. Lowering their tail segment, they swooped down over the water and deposited tens of thousands of chartreuse eggs, which afterwards, looked like miniature landing strips. Tens of thousands seems like an excessive number of eggs per dragonfly, until you see the throngs of frogs and turtles that gulp them up like insatiable herpetological vacuum cleaners.

I tried to home in on a particularly big-faced dragonfly as it skimmed over the water, but my eye simply couldn't keep up with its erratic, fizzling-firework movements. After about a minute, I noticed that the dragonfly's flight pattern involved a predictable, albeit jagged, circular route over the pond: a straight sprint to the right, a zigzag low over the water, a curlicue in the distance, a straight sprint and a dart-dart-dart to my left, and then finally, a long hover in front of me. "Wait . . . did it just look at me?" I thought. Around the jagged loop it went. Again, it stared me down with those crazed eyes. We scanned each other, and I knew *it* had the upper hand—it gleaned way more information about me than I did it. Each time it zipped past to resume its circuit, it hovered a little closer.

I was giddy. My best chance of getting a shot was during a hovering maneuver, when I could see details in its pea-sized face, including its bulbous blue eyes and high-sheen white mouth. Raising my camera in anticipation of its arrival became part of *my* routine, but the dragonfly inevitably sped away before I could find it in my lens. It raced and darted around its established route, always pausing to hover before continuing on. Dragonflies are reliable. My timing was not.

Eventually, I could anticipate where it would be two seconds before it got there. My finger twitched on the release button as the dragonfly swung around the final curve. My blue-eyed friend zipped in front of me and I clicked off two shots before it took off again. I was flabbergasted by what I saw in my playback screen: a perfectly in-focus, blue and green, hovering dragonfly, a darner. Around it went, and this time, it hovered sideways, as if posing for me. I got shots of its blue, green, and brown mosaic tail and striped thorax, which reminded me of intricate Italian mosaic.

I learned that dragons have what's called compound eyes; the true eyes are three black dots between the big shiny spheres I loved so much. I was determined to find as many as possible before winter came.

Something red darted out from under my boot. Landing in a patch of sun ahead of me on the path, it lifted its wings high above its body and plopped them down on the dirt—*whomp!* The dragonfly looked like it had been dipped in firetruck-red paint. Eyes, thorax, tail, legs, hairs on the legs, and even the veins in its wings: they were all red. When I moved in closer, it took off like a toy helicopter. Then it landed in the next patch of sun. Slowly, I drew the shadow of my arm across the red beauty. It darted back to the original sunny patch behind me, and down went the wings—*whomp!* It didn't mind my being there, it just didn't like my shadow. There were more Cardinal Meadowhawks along the path; some on the ground, and one pretending to be a leaf on the tip of a bare branch. Sallying out over water or grass, they returned with delicate little wings poking out of their mouths.

I'm particularly fond of Western Pondhawks. When illuminated by the sun, female pondhawks look like green glass. Males are coated in a light blue, chalky substance called pruinose white, which supposedly makes female pondhawks go berserk sexually.

One day, I witnessed a female pondhawk snag a male Tule Bluet Damselfly midair. The pondhawk landed, prey in mouth, on a tree trunk, where the damselfly was firmly pinned down against the bark. It must've taken a full thirty seconds for the pondhawk to fully extend its powerful mandibles, which opened so wide, they looked unhinged. It only took a second to chomp down on the bluet's neck, which left its tiny blue head dangling freakishly to one side. The dragonfly devoured its smaller cousin in ultra-slow motion. It was truly grizzly to witness the bluet's blue-and-black-striped, wide-eyed face as its body parts gradually disappeared into the jaws of the glow stick-green pondhawk. The last morsel to go down the dragon's gullet was the damsel's tiny O-shaped mouth.

ঌ

Like mating hummingbirds, saddlebags soar straight overhead. Once I developed the ability to spot them, I noticed them everywhere, even in my front yard. My peripheral brain must've been deciphering them as horse flies or those black floaty things that travel around in your eyeballs.

The inkblot-like Black Saddlebag Dragonfly is monochrome, like the red Cardinal Meadowhawk, or Aunt Helen's pink bathroom. My favorite detail was the jellybean-shaped spaces between the black saddlebags and tail where blue pokes through—a tattoo on an azure blue sky.

Part Fourteen

The Buffer Zone

There's a photo of me playing piano when I was three years old. It's a black and white, but I have a clear memory of the ruffled pink dress I was wearing. My legs dangle from the bench and cross nonchalantly at the ankle. My fingers splay over the keys. My face frowns in concentration, and my expression says, "Don't bother me, Dad. I'm practicing."

Now, in 2015, fifty-seven years later, I'm sitting at the Oregon Symphony's 9-foot Steinway. I'm in my performance blacks, in my comfort zone at the back of the orchestra. My hands hover, poised over the keys and ready to play. I'm aware of the natural shape of my hands—mountain ranges. A thrill of anticipation blossoms in my chest.

The conductor strikes a pose as he performs for the audience. I mumble to myself, "Okay, you're stunningly charismatic. . . . Now how about a downbeat? Ah . . . there it is!"

As the pianist in the orchestra, I have a built-in buffer zone from violinists, harpists, horn players, and percussionists who threaten to infringe on my psychic and physical space. Even so, it's not always enough. A conductor's energy can travel great distances, even to the far reaches of the stage. Constant vigilance is required to keep tethered to my innate musicality—it is, after all, why I was hired. Being a musician is supposed to be about more than just correct notes and rhythms. I conjure my roots and sense the presence of peaceful concentration. Memories surface: Mr. Raieff's glimmering eyes, Anne Koscielny's belly laugh, burnt orange light sweeping over the northern landscape, the tap of Beethoven's fingers on the armrest, the delicately intricate wing of a dragonfly, the bosom-hug of my grandmother, the intensity of my father's unwavering love.

My fingers say, "We know what we're doing. Just let me play."

Codetta

My father's been gone for thirty years, and the snapshot of our hands playing side by side is still vibrant in my memory. So much of my childhood lies beneath rock—beyond my consciousness's reach. Yet, I have this river, this gift, this thing that nourishes and fuels me every day. I can't imagine what it would be like to reflect on my life without the river of music.

Before he died, my father left me a note. I keep it hanging on the pegboard in my office. It says,

Dearest Carol—
You will never be
alone
because god is
everywhere

and my love will
always be with you.

Dad

He was right.

Made in the USA
Monee, IL
30 March 2021

64269967R00134